OF PEATS AND

OF PEATS AND PUTTS
DOWN UNDER

EXPLORING WHISKY AND GOLF IN AUSTRALIA AND NEW ZEALAND

ANDREW BROWN

YOUCAXTON
PUBLICATIONS

Contents

Andrew Brown was born in Edinburgh, brought up in the Borders and educated at Loretto School in Musselburgh. After reading history at Cambridge University, he pursued a career in the food industry, marketing many famous brands such as Bisto, Hovis and Mr Kipling. He has three grown-up children and is now retired and living in Cornwall. Apart from playing golf – he enjoys playing over the links at both St Enodoc and Perranporth as well as making regular pilgrimages to his native Scotland - he enjoys dog walking, occasional games of tennis and developing his Cornish garden.

For my sister, Lucy, who helped and guided me
on my Australasian adventures

King Island

Cape Wickham

Ocean Dunes

Fannys Bay

Barnbougle

Hellyers Road

Tasmania

Waubs Harbour

Callington Mill

Ratho Farm

Lark

Hobart

New Zealand

90 Mile Beach Kauri Cliffs
Waitangi
Te Arai
Waiheke
Waiheke

Pokeno

Wairekei

Takaka
Kiwi Spirits
Paraparaumu Beach

Reefton

Hokitika

Wanaka
Cardrona
Arrowtown
Jack's Point
Whisky Galore
Spirits Workshop

NZWC

Chisholm Links

PREFACE

OF PEATS AND Putts' global ambitions knows no bounds. Many friends and colleagues have asked where my next destination would be to continue my quest exploring how whisky and golf have developed around the world. The initial foray to England, Wales and Ireland was predictable, the more extensive trips around continental Europe perhaps a little more surprising. Having returned in my fourth book to my native Scotland, I felt it was time to extend my wings and look beyond western Europe. The two most obvious candidates were North America and Japan. The United States is the biggest export market for Single Malt Scotch and also has a thriving whiskey and bourbon industry (indeed the differences between whiskey and bourbon would make for some interesting comparisons) and America has since the Great War in many ways dominated the world of golf. Many Scots have contributed to the development of whisky and particularly golf in the United States – Jim Beam and Maker's Mark have Scots who played an important role in their development while many of the great early courses in the U.S. were designed by the likes of Donald Ross, Willie Park Junior and others Scots emigrés. On the other hand, from the 1920s, Japan also took to both golf and whisky with many of the country's top golf courses and whisky distilleriesdating from then.The English architect Charles Allison designed Naruo in 1930, the same year that Abiko Golf Club was founded while Suntory's Yamazaki Distillery was opened by Shinjiro Torii in 1923 and Masataka Taketsuru set up Yoichi distillery near Hoikkado in 1934. Taketsuru had studied organic chemistry at Glasgow University and spent a number of years working at Scottish distilleries having married a Scot and lived in Campbeltown. Japanese malt whisky was the first outside of Scotland and Ireland to gain a strong international reputation.

There would certainly be enough material for volumes on both countries, or continents if you extended to Canada for North America and to Asia for Japan, where the likes of Kavalan in Taiwan and Amrut in India are becoming well-known names. In fact, for me there would probably be too much material for someone who essentially prefers interesting niches. I am not in the business of writing definitive studies of whisky and golf in a particular country but rather sharing personal observations and experiences. This leads to the main problem: so many of the famous golf courses in the U.S. and, to some extent also in Japan, are private members' clubs and you cannot just turn up, pay a green fee and play. For my purposes, I want golf courses and whisky distilleries which are accessible to everyone. In Scotland, I reckon only about three or four of the top hundred courses are not easily accessible and, even if many today have become very expensive, you can still play them; this is not the case in the U.S.

So, I turned my attentions elsewhere. I had twice visited Australia where my youngest sister had lived for over thirty years. I knew that there was some interesting golfing history and I remembered reading, while researching my first book, about a Tasmanian whisky winning 'World Whisky of the Year' in 2014 and causing something of a stir. I had also on my second trip to Australia spent three days in Tasmania playing Barnbougle Dunes and had vowed to return. And finally, I had always wanted to visit New Zealand where I knew about some famous old courses and had been reading about many new ones as well as some early signs of a developing whisky industry. So, Australasia it was.

But even then, I decided to focus. Australia is vast and I have decided to concentrate on Tasmania – as I say, I like niches, though Tasmania in the context of the Australian whisky industry is much more than a niche. It is Australia's smallest state by size with just 2% of the country's population but arguably can be regarded as the heart of the country's whisky industry and can boast over a quarter of the country's whisky distilleries. It also has probably three of the five top golf courses in the country. Before going to New Zealand, I decided to have one chapter on Melbourne and Sydney where there is a lot of golfing history which I think adds context. I didn't explore much whisky in those cities but as they dominate Australia and are home to about 40% of the country's total population, they are likely to feature in many of the larger whisky developments.

Having decided that my focus would be on Tasmania and New Zealand, I had to consider the format. My previous books had comfortably suited having nine chapters, each visiting a whisky and a golfing location. In the UK it is easy to find golf courses and whisky distilleries relatively nearby. In Europe, I expanded my definition of proximate (in Germany it meant over 1,000 kilometres apart but in the same country) but I kept to my familiar format. I soon decided that sticking to it this time would be an uncomfortable constraint and so I have made three changes; there are eighteen chapters rather than nine (I wanted to stick to a golfing number though interestingly on this trip I played a number of courses with neither nine nor eighteen holes), some chapters will be either golf only or whisky only and the chapters will be of markedly different lengths. Yes, there will be some short par 3s and long Par 5s and Par 4s of different lengths.

Finally, I think that there will be more about the places I visited. At times the book is a bit of a travelogue but this reflects my journey; I was researching this book but I was also visiting most places for the first time as a tourist and wanted to reflect on that. For those who have not visited any of the places, I hope that you are inspired to do so – I'm giving nothing away in saying that both Tasmania and New Zealand are remarkable places with some extraordinary scenery.

As you know, I like context and I will start with some facts which helped me put these visits into context. Tasmania has the same population as Cornwall where I now enjoy living as it is much less crowded than the south-east of England where I used to live. However, the area of Tasmania is twenty times the size of Cornwall. Tasmania, with under 600,000 people is nearly as big as the island of Ireland, which has seven million people. New Zealand has the same population as Scotland but is over 3.5 times its size. These are vast countries with relatively small populations and most of those populations are concentrated in the few cities. It takes someone from the U.K. a little time to comprehend.

While the vastness and emptiness can sound attractive, it does bring challenges for both golf and whisky. How can you provide excellence in both without scale? It is the same challenge that faces island communities in Scotland and some of the more isolated golf clubs. A golf club needs members and/or regular visitors to generate income to maintain a quality course and clubhouse facilities – if it is located in an isolated community this can be difficult. Start-up whisky distilleries in Tasmania have a local market of under 600,000 people compared to over five million in Scotland or seven million in Ireland, not to mention nearly seventy million in the U.K.

It is also worth saying how recent some of the developments have been. I started working on my first book around 2015, less than ten years ago. Five of the eighteen golf courses I feature here did not exist then and only one of the whisky distilleries I visited in Tasmania and none of the ones in New Zealand. Every year, I buy Ingvar Ronde's magnificent Malt Whisky Yearbook, which has served as my 'Bible' for what is happening around the world of malt whisky. The first one I bought was in 2015 and listed fourteen businesses in Australia and just two in New Zealand. The 2025 copy has ninety entries for Australia and twelve for New Zealand. I have talked about the explosion in new distilleries in Scotland and Ireland (and indeed continental Europe) but Australia and New Zealand have been no different.

I embarked on this quest, as usual, with no great knowledge, just a feel that there was much to explore, and I was not disappointed. Don't expect any great conclusions or detailed analysis of either 'industry' but plenty of observations from an interested amateur which I hope will tempt you to explore further for yourself.

The rural charm of Ratho Farm

The River Clyde is very much in play

CHAPTER 1

BOTHWELL

BOTHWELL SEEMS TO be an ideal place to begin my antipodean adventure looking into Scotland's two great exports, whisky and golf. The name Bothwell is perhaps most commonly associated in Scottish history with the Earl of Bothwell, the third husband of Mary Queen of Scots, who was implicated in the murder of her previous husband, Lord Darnley. Bothwell is also an historic village in Lanarkshire with a famous 13th century castle which was laid to siege by Edward 1st in 1301 during the wars of independence. It was also the scene of the Battle of Bothwell Bridge in 1679 between the Presbyterian Covenanters and Government forces led by the notorious Duke of Monmouth following the restoration of Charles II.

Bothwell, Tasmania, was named after this village around the 1820s when several families of Scottish origin settled in the area. It sits on a river with an equally familiar name: the Clyde. It is perhaps not surprising, therefore, that it is the location of Australia's oldest golf course and the Australasian Golf Museum. However, what is truly serendipitous is that it was also the location for the birth, or rather 'rebirth', of the Tasmanian whisky industry some thirty-five years ago.

In 1989, Bill Lark, a land surveyor from Hobart, went trout fishing on the river Clyde in the Central Highlands of Tasmania with his father-in-law, Max. One evening, accompanied by their wives, as they set up a barbecue in a park in Bothwell, Max produced a bottle of

Single Malt Scotch Whisky. As they enjoyed this treat, Bill pondered why no one was making whisky in Tasmania. It was a good question because, as he pointed out, there were good water supplies, plentiful quality barley and a climate not dissimilar to that in Scotland. There were even peat bogs.

The answer to the question was simple: Tasmania had had some sixteen distilleries in the 1820s and 1830s but distilling had been outlawed in 1839 by Sir John Franklin, the Governor of Van Diemen's Land, as Tasmania was then called, allegedly on the prompting of his puritan-minded wife, Lady Jane. 150 years later the ban was, to all intents and purposes, still in place. Before anyone could start a Tasmanian distillery, the first task was to get the prohibition over-turned and Bill and his wife Lyn found to their surprise that there was plenty of political support for this. By 1992 the legislation had been amended allowing small scale distilling and enabling start-up whisky distilleries to be established. Just over thirty years later, there are now over seventy whisky distilleries in Tasmania which has become 'the Speyside' of the Australian whisky industry. Bill Lark and other members of his family have been involved in many of these new distilleries and he is now regarded as the 'Father' of the Tasmanian industry.

If there is a 'Father' of today's Tasmanian golf scene it is perhaps Greg Ramsay. He was brought up on Ratho Farm in Bothwell which had been bought by his great-grandfather and he has not only been instrumental in the restoration of the Ratho Farm course but he also provided the inspiration for Barnbougle Dunes, the remarkable golfing destination on Tasmania's north-east coast where we will be headed quite soon. Conveniently for my purposes, Greg has also been involved in a number of whisky projects, both in Tasmania and New Zealand so his name will appear again. Indeed, Greg Ramsay can be said to have been involved in numerous golf and whisky projects all over the world, though not all of them successful.

The story of Bothwell starts in 1822 when Alexander Reid of Ratho Bank Estate near Edinburgh and a merchant in the port of Leith, emigrated to the new Van Diemens Land on the merchant ship, *Castle Forbes*, with a group of other east-coast emigrés. Reid was granted 1,400 acres of land on the Clyde River in what was then the remote Central Highlands north of Hobart and together with the other, mainly Scottish, settlers in the area he helped establish the small town which became Bothwell. Reid established a successful Merino sheep farm on his land, producing fine wool and selling breeding stock to other settlers and named it Ratho Farm. At some stage in the ensuing decades, he laid out some golf holes and invited friends and neighbours to play golf.

The debate as to the oldest golf course outside Scotland is a difficult one to determine but I think Royal Calcutta in 1829 probably has the strongest claim. A formal golf club was also established at Pau in France in 1856 and there is evidence that golf had been played there for many years before. In fact, the second Alexander Reid's greatest claim to sporting fame was probably bringing the 1882 Melbourne Cup winner, The Assyrian, to stud. Bothwell Golf Club at Ratho Farm was not formally established until 1902, relatively late and certainly after the likes of The Australian Golf Club in Sydney, founded in 1882, and Royal Melbourne in 1891. The first Golf Club founded in New Zealand, as we will learn, was the Otago Golf Club in Dunedin in 1871. We should be clear therefore that we are talking about the oldest golf 'course' not club.

The Reids had returned for a few years to Edinburgh in the late 1830s to educate their children, returning in 1842, and it is most likely that it is around this time that a 'golf course' of some sort was laid out. Alexander Reid III, who was born in 1861 and lived until the age of ninety-nine recounted to a historian that he remembered old golf clubs being kept in long boxes in what must have been the early 1870s. Early records from Bothwell Golf Club suggest that indeed by the end of the century a number of local farms (Logan, Cluny and Hartfield) had 'golf courses' on their landholdings and informal competitions would rotate between these venues.

Alexander Reid III sold the farm in 1935 to Alexander Stenhouse, the grandfather of Greg Ramsay's mother, Mary Ramsay, and it has stayed in the family since. Today the venue is marketed as a 'boutique accommodation, golf, wedding and function venue'. It does not have a luxury corporate feel, rather it relies on old-world charm and the same can be said about the golf course. This is not a top-class golf course by any stretch of the imagination but it oozes history and character. You don't visit Ratho Farm to play a great golf course; you visit to immerse yourself in the game's origins and enjoy the distinctive quirkiness of the course. That is not to say that it doesn't offer some challenging golf; it certainly does but it is more fun than golf-course design excellence.

As I have said, the history of the course is somewhat patchy. When it was set up by Alexander Reid some reports suggest there were only two holes. This was increased to twelve at some stage but six of these were lost after the second World War and more recently newer holes have been laid out around the homestead. In 2014, following study of old aerial pictures and scorecards, six of the original holes on the town side of the homestead close to the river Clyde were restored and opened with a hickory club challenge match involving a number of Australia's golfing greats. Certainly these 'new old' holes now provide some of the best challenges.

It is worth talking through the layout and some of the holes to give a flavour of the experience. I hired clubs – all my golf in this book was played with hired clubs, something I will discuss later – but I decided to play with conventional modern ones rather than hickories. When I say 'modern', they were probably late 20th rather than 21st century but I had no complaints. The 1st tee is situated right in front of the homestead where I had been met by a very enthusiastic Argentinian lady who was new to the job and not that familiar with golf, but she managed to take my modest green fee and find me some clubs. She had pointed to the 1st tee but I have to say that having got there I wasn't sure where to go. I even looked in both directions but as there was a large green behind me (it transpired that this was both the putting green and the 18th green) it seemed that I was required to hit over a couple of fences, presumably between the two farm sheds. The scorecard suggested it was a Par 3 of only some 180 yards but I could see neither a flag nor a green.

I often like to talk you through some of my shots – memorable ones and there will be some which I will describe later in this book. Long putts that go in, 3 woods that never leave the line of the pin. I'm already itching to tell you about the 1st hole at Paraparaumu Beach. But I should really also describe my first shot at Ratho Farm. I decided that because I really had no idea where I was going to take a small rescue club which might not go 180 yards but would find somewhere safe over the second fence. Before describing the shot, I should preface matters by saying that this was my first swing of a golf club since arriving in Australia some forty-eight hours previously. I'm not sure whether I swung too fast or too slowly or whether I lifted my head in anxiety because I frankly had no clue where I was going. But the ball failed to rise more than a few feet off the ground and dived just over the first fence and into very thick long grass and scrub just by the second fence. There was no prospect of finding it. My second, even more cautious attempt, went high and slightly right (in cricketing terminology, a skied off-drive which would have been caught at cover point) and I set off through the two wooden gates. It was not a propitious start.

I found my second ball lying in the open though not exactly in the right direction but I was on my way. Let us say that this is a hole which is better played the second time around. The second hole is another Par 3 of similar distance, played almost directly over the 1st green and gently uphill towards some farm buildings. Both the 1st and 2nd greens are distinctively square making them easy to fence off from sheep. There were no fences when I played but having played Brora I am not unfamiliar with this practice.

Holes 3-8 are the new restored holes situated on the Bothwell town side of the farmstead. To find the 3rd tee you have to walk through the farm and when you get there again you wonder again whether you are in the right place. Am I really supposed to hit directly over that large cattle yard? The answer is yes. It's a Par 5 which sweeps left to right and down towards the river. If you successfully negotiate the cattle yard, there is plenty of room. It's a pleasingly shaped hole, a gentle left-to-right dog-leg across the road into the homestead and down to the green which is set beside the Clyde river. The 4th is a tough Par 3 of nearly two hundred yards played parallel to the river – you obviously mustn't go right. The next challenge is to find the 5th tee. There is a small wooden bridge over the river and a sign indicating the next tee. Suffice to say that there are a few options through the bushes when you cross the river but eventually I climbed a bank and found a teeing area with a view through the bushes back over to the course on the other side of the river. Again, you hit without the reassurance that you really know where you should be going but I hit a nice strike up the left but into what looked like a good position. It is not a long hole and it turned out that my drive was in 'Position A' and I had a short iron into the green. Holes 6 and 7 then play towards the river and back to the road respectively and 8 delivers another slightly alarming tee shot where you have to hit over a hedge seemingly into the farmyard where the green is tucked away in the corner. You certainly feel as if you are more in a farmyard than on a golf course on this hole.

Holes 9-14 are then laid out on a large expanse of land to the east of the property. There is much more space here though the dry hard surfaces of the fairways when I played meant that you had to be careful to watch how the ball bounced. Some of these holes have been re-formatted: 12 and 14 are Par 5s, while 11, which abuts the main road, is a short par 4 up to a green in the corner of the homestead from where there is a fine view back across the course.

The 14th green returns you to near the first hole from where you walk back past the 1st tee to the final section of the course which again has its own peculiar characteristics. If you had just got used to opening your shoulders for holes 9-14, it's time to rein in your ambitions as this final section requires much greater accuracy. 15 is a Par 5 where you drive through a disconcertingly narrow gap in the trees and the second shot at the Par 5 requires you to lay up short of the river. You play your third over the attractive bullrushes and the river to a small green surrounded by trouble. 16 is a great short par 4 with two fairway options; either drive across the river to the left from where you will have a relatively easy pitch or stay to the right of the river and hit your pitch over it. Neither option is easy. 17 is a tough long Par 3 before you return home on 18, a long, narrow right to left Par 5 where your third shot is over a high hedge hidden behind which is the 18th green. There is a degree of 'crazy golf' about this but why not? Golf is meant to be fun.

**The 18th green is approached either over
or through this gap in the hedge**

It's hard to categorise Ratho Farm as a golf course. Frankly it will never make it into the Top 100 rankings in Australia but that is not the point. In some ways it comprises a hotch potch of holes though there are a number which arguably have architectural merit. I think 3, 4, and 5 are excellent holes while 15 and 16 are terrifying but require accurate shot making. The quality of the course is pretty variable but that is understandable when there is not the scale of members or visitors to generate income to sustain a regular green-keeping staff. This is an issue we will discover particularly in New Zealand. When the eighteen holes were reopened in 2018, a number of Australia's golfing greats came along. Probably the greatest of them all, Peter Thomson, five times winner of The Open, summed it up rather well. *'It's historic. It doesn't pretend to be anything it's not. It's an important part of the game of golf. It's holy.'* I couldn't put it better myself.

That is the point about Ratho Farm – you don't go there for golfing excellence but for a golfing experience. It has a real claim to be where the first golf holes were laid out in Australia and to be able to play eighteen holes there today over that same land is what is important. The fact that the golf course is played through a farmstead is recognition of its roots, its history. We don't go there for a carefully designed golf course with manicured fairways and greens. We go there to experience and feel the history which oozes from the place. Some of the holes, as I have said, are rather good and some are either totally unremarkable or perhaps a bit silly. But that doesn't matter.

Ratho Farm markets itself as offering, in addition to golf and trout fishing, luxury boutique accommodation. From my quick look at it I'm not sure how luxury it is (I always think 'boutique' is a clever word that really doesn't define anything when related to accommodation) but again that is not the point. The website talks of an 'experience steeped in heritage and natural splendour' and that is definitely the case.

There is a connection between Ratho Farm and a whisky distillery but this gets us into a murky story which I will only attempt to summarise. The Nant Whisky Distillery was a neighbour to Ratho Farm and was set up in 2007 by Keith Batt with the first whisky produced in 2011. It soon gained a strong international reputation and won a number of awards. It then set up a barrel investment scheme – not an unusual activity for a new cash-hungry whisky business needing to lay down new stock. Unfortunately, things soon started to go wrong, with Nant's owner being declared bankrupt as a result of another investment and it started to become clear that there were more barrel investors than barrels of whisky. At this stage the distillery was bought by Australian Whisky Holdings who discovered the extent of the problem. I am not going to try and explain exactly what happened – it ultimately involved many lawsuits, claims and counter-claims – nor to comment on it though it is clear that many investors lost out and this damaged the reputation of barrel investment schemes which are an important source of capital for start-up businesses in the growing whisky market. Australian Whisky Holdings then went on to buy Lark Distillery and invest in a new distillery site at Pontville north of Hobart.

Nant and Ratho Farm could therefore be an excellent combination to start my Tasmanian whisky and golf adventure but the Nant scandal (I think this is an appropriate word) prevents it being so. As we will see there is so much to admire in the Tasmanian whisky industry but sadly that does not include the Nant story. Instead, we will move on in the next chapter to a much more positive story which has taken place in another small town in the Central Highlands of Tasmania, just some forty kilometres to the east.

The impressive still house at Callington Mill

The beautifully restored flour mill at Callington Mill

CHAPTER 2

OATLANDS

I HAD FLOWN into Hobart, the capital of Tasmania with some 200,000 inhabitants, and while it doesn't feature any of my chosen golf and whisky destinations, it deserves at least a mention in passing. It has a picturesque waterfront and there is plenty to see and do from the wonderful Botanic Gardens to the avant-garde MONA Museum. The harbour is the starting point for many trips to the likes of the beautiful Bruny Island or the historic Port Arthur and other destinations on the Tasman Peninsula. Unsurprisingly it remains an important hub for the Tasmanian whisky industry. As well as many whisky bars, it is the home of Sullivan's Cove which gave the industry an enormous boost by winning the World's Best Single Malt at the World Whiskies Awards in 2014. Like Sullivan's Cove the original Lark Distillery is in the Hobart suburb of Cambridge, though visitors to Lark are now directed to the newly acquired Shene Distillery at Pontville. The other brand worthy of mention is Overeem, situated in the suburb of Richmond (yes, Hobart suburbs often have familiar names to British visitors). All these businesses have their own stories of entrepreneurial start-ups which have fuelled the growth of the industry. On my first night in Hobart, I found a whisky bar and was astonished to count on the menu some thirty different Tasmanian whisky brands. When I then met and talked to players in the industry, I discovered that there were probably over double that number of distilleries now operating on the island.

Hobart is perhaps less of a golfing destination, with the two main courses, The Tasmania and Royal Hobart, being good if not great courses and clubs. More interesting is a new project at 7 Mile Beach just east of the city where a public links is being built. I visited the site and it is certainly a glorious one for a golf course. The project was the inspiration of a PGA Tour professional Mathew Goggin who grew up in the area and recognised the potential of the site. He eventually teamed up with the architect Michael Clayton who was involved with Tom Doak in the original design of Barnbougle Dunes. The course is still not open at time of writing and has been subject to a number of delays, but with its vision of a world-class traditional golfing venue open to the public and sharing the natural environment with 'walkers, horse riders, dog walkers and beach goers' I hope that it is a success.

There is another proposed development at Arm End, further down the Tasman Peninsula. Here, initial planning permission was received as long ago as 2015 with construction at one time due to begin in 2020 but at time of writing there are still appeals in play with The Tasman Conservation Trust among others opposed to the scheme. I don't have enough knowledge to comment; sometimes golf courses, if constructed sympathetically, can actually contribute to the maintenance of a special environment but I can understand the caution on what is clearly a sensitive site.

I drove up to Oatlands from 7 Mile Beach through the attractive Coal Valley. It doesn't take long for you to leave Hobart's suburbs and find yourself in vast sweeping countryside. Oatlands is attractively situated on Lake Dulverton in the Central Highlands just off Highway 1, the main arterial road up the centre of Tasmania linking Hobart with Launceston, the second city. If anything, Oatlands is even more attractive and has perhaps a more prosperous feeling than Bothwell with some noteworthy Georgian (yes, Georgian as the settlement dates from the 1820s) architecture. Indeed, it is said to have the largest collection of sandstone Georgian buildings in Australia as well as the beautiful St Pauls' Catholic Church which was designed by Augustus Pugin of Big Ben fame. One of the small town's many prominent buildings is Callington Mill, Australia's third oldest windmill dating from 1837, and it is there that one of Tasmania's and Australia's newest and biggest whisky distilleries has been built.

I like distilleries with stories and the story of Callington Mill is an extraordinary one. It also epitomises the cooperative culture of the Tasmanian whisky industry which will be an important factor in its success. The story includes many of the great names in the industry including Bill Lark himself, Damien Mackay, another of the early pioneers of Tasmanian Whisky, and John Ibrahim, an entrepreneur and successful businessman who became a friend of Bill Lark, gained a passion for Tasmanian whisky and had a vision for how to build the industry. A growing industry also needs investment and John brought in investment partners, twin brothers Salim and Danny Nicolas.

It's a story of friendships and business deals which, as is also often the case in the whisky industry in Scotland, is at times complicated. The details don't matter a lot but I will try and summarise my understanding of them. The story starts back in 2015 when John Ibrahim, a businessman from Sydney, bought Dysart House in Kempton less than half an hour from Oatlands. He bought it as a holiday home – at that time he had no interest in or knowledge of whisky. It transpired that at the same time Bill Lark had also been looking at Dysart House as a possible location for one of his distillery interests, Redlands Distillery, which needed to relocate. They were introduced by the land agent and this serendipitous meeting led John

Ibrahim to invest with Bill in setting up The Old Kempton Distillery on the site of the house. The following year he and Bill Lark took a trip to Scotland and it was this that proved to be the real inspiration for what became Callington Mill. Bill was already well respected within the Scottish industry and able to introduce John to many of the movers and shakers. That same year John, with his investment partners Salim and Danny, invested in The Shene Distillery at Pontville with the estate owners, the Kernke family, and Damien Mackay who had been distilling in Tasmania for nearly a decade. This distillery was developed and then sold to Lark (by this time owned by Australian Whisky Holdings) which needed the capacity and this enabled John Ibrahim to turn his attention to creating his vision of a new, turnkey Tasmanian Whisky Distillery.

**Visitors are greeted with this
oversize deck chair**

The site he chose was Callington Mill in Oatlands. The history of the mill is also interesting as it was set up by a settler from Cornwall, John Vincent, who in many respects was the John Ibrahim of two hundred years previously. He had emigrated with his wife Susannah from Callington in Cornwall and initially set up as a publican in Bothwell. An entrepreneur, he went on to develop other pubs and hotels before developing Callington Mill in 1837 in nearby Oatlands. Evidence suggests that he used milled grains to produce illegal whisky to supply his pubs. Rather like the new whisky distillery, the flour mill used what was at the time state-of-the-art technology using two pairs of French burr stones powered by shuttered sails that could be opened and closed by pulling outside chains. A steam driven mill was added later. Today it has been completely restored and is the only functioning Lincolnshire-style windmill in the southern hemisphere. I briefly worked in the flour milling industry in the U.K. and visiting the mill I could sense how excited my ex-flour-milling production and engineering colleagues would be at the sight of this restored gem.

Callington Mill is important in the story of the development of Tasmanian Whisky for a number of reasons. First, it was the first scale operator to build a new turnkey distillery using Tasmanian suppliers. This may not seem that significant but a few years ago this would not have been possible – indeed one of the constraints to the growth of the industry was the lack of suppliers of process equipment. The explosion of new distillery start-ups across the world has seen lead times for the supply of distillery equipment get longer, to the frustration of many whisky entrepreneurs. John Ibrahim's vision was of a brand-new state-of-the-art distillery so he needed a 'turnkey' solution and initially he worked with Forsyths in Scotland as well as Italian and German suppliers as they were the only options available.

But he didn't like the concept of a new flagship Tasmanian Distillery being built with Scottish or Italian equipment. This was when he approached a company in Westbury in Northern Tasmania called Kolmark, a producer of stainless-steel process equipment. One of its co-founders, Mark Kolodziej, recognised the potential market for supplying turnkey solutions to new whisky businesses and took a trip with John Ibrahim to Cardrona near Queenstown in New Zealand where a new distillery had recently been built. We will visit Cardrona in Chapter 11. The result of this trip was that Kolmark started a new business stream and John Ibrahim got his vision for Callington Mill to become Tasmania's first scale turnkey new distillery using Tasmanian equipment and Tasmanian engineering expertise. A burgeoning new industry requires not just whisky enthusiast entrepreneurs but also those who will supply the necessary infrastructure.

The second point about Callington Mill is the scale it brings to the industry. 500,000 litres is big in the context of the Tasmanian industry – it is bigger than many of the new start-ups in Scotland – and this will help fulfil some of the pent-up demand that Tasmanian whisky is experiencing as well as enabling a competitive pricing strategy. Typically, Callington Mill products are priced below the likes of Lark and Sullivan's Cove with entry prices below $150 and premium expressions selling at around $200. Most Lark, Sullivan's Cove and indeed Overeem products are about $200 and above.

The scale of the operation does not imply that this has been at the expense of quality, quite the contrary. Everything at Callington Mill has been engineered for quality – it is clear from the moment that you enter the car park that no expense has been spared. Whisky is not an investment for those who want a quick pay back. The old buildings have been lovingly restored – you can visit the magnificent flour mill – while the new distillery buildings and visitor centre ooze quality. The restaurant is exceptional and it is no surprise to learn that it was awarded Visitor Attraction of the Year at the 2024 Icons of Whisky Awards.

A quick word on terminology: distillery visits in Australia and New Zealand are called 'Cellar Door'. This obviously reflects that both countries are more famous for their wine and the growth of vineyards as visitor attractions. Whisky distilleries have adopted the same terminology with some building the offering into their business plans. These Cellar Door experiences vary in scope and price from a distillery visit, a self-guided tour and/or a hosted tasting. Some will have cafés or, as at Callington Mill, a fine restaurant. Lark has a 'Cellar Door' in central Hobart, separate from its distillery, which is effectively just a shop and a bar but there will be staff to talk you through the various products.

On the product, the business philosophy is also not to take short cuts and indeed to follow Scotch Whisky standards. Australian Whisky still has less rigorous standards than Scotch and there is a debate within The Tasmanian Whisky and Spirits Association as to whether they should tighten the standards for Tasmanian whisky. As the number of distilleries has leapt from about eight to around eighty over the past fifteen years there is something to be said for that. Suffice to say that Callington Mill would be in favour of tightening the standards.

As well as state-of-the-art mashing, fermentation and distilling equipment, Callington Mill has its own cooperage and alliances with cooperages in Spain and Portugal. The primary casks are not ex-bourbon but wine barrels from the Douro in Portugal and sherry casks from Spain plus some Australian fortified wine barrels. They are also using a Solera blending system comprising fourteen casks to produce premium expressions. I am not best placed to comment on whisky styles but my impression is that Callington Mill produces rich-tasting, quite vinious whiskies which would seem to concur with the maturation strategy. As with all new whisky businesses there will also be experimentation (casks from other countries) and a number of different ranges. This was, however, the first time I had seen finished whisky stored in terracotta!

I was shown around by Rizk Mawass, the General Manager, whose infectious enthusiasm for the business and pride in what had been achieved in a relatively short time was shared by all the other employees I met. The new distillery is clearly important to the town and it sees itself as an important part of the local community – the location is part of its identity as is so often the case with whisky. As an indication, they have launched a limited-edition Heritage Series of cask-strength bottlings, featuring sketches by John Ibrahim's wife of various historic buildings in Oatlands. Clearly the scale will build over the coming years – warehousing for maturation has been built on the edge of the town.

Callington Mill is poised to become a major player in Tasmania due to its scale, its innovation and the fact that it seems well funded. Developing industries need businesses like it.

Time was pressing so I was unable to play Oatlands Golf Club, situated on the edge of the town, but I did visit it briefly. Some locals will maintain that it actually pre-dates Bothwell as a formal golf club. It is an attractive small nine-hole course (most reviews mention the abundant wildlife) with an unassuming clubhouse but looks to be an important part of the community. As such it reflects many such small courses in Tasmania – enjoying golf in Tasmania, as in Scotland, is not just about visiting the famous top venues.

The stills at Waubs Harbour

Waubs Harbour Distillery is on the site of an old oyster hatchery

CHAPTER 3

FREYCINET AND BICHENO

FROM OATLANDS I headed for the east coast. I decided to join the A3 Tasman Highway which starts from Hobart and hits the east coast at the pretty town of Orford before heading north. You need to be careful in Tasmania if taking short-cuts on roads which digital-mapping devices might recommend, as you may find yourself on dirt tracks where 10mph/15kph is your top speed. What looks like a short cut may cost you quite a lot of time. The east coast Tasman Highway is, however, good and, like most of Tasmania most of the time, very quiet. I was there in the height of summer (late January, early February) and everywhere the vegetation was lush. I need to talk about agapanthus. Having recently moved to Cornwall, I thought I knew a bit about the glories of agapanthus. I have some in my garden there and have ordered more because I find it an uplifting plant. But in Tasmania they are everywhere. And I mean *everywhere* with white ones competing with the more usual blue or purple ones. They are in gardens, in the streets, growing wild along the sides of the roads. They are glorious but after a few days I was beginning to get symptons of 'agapanthus overload'. I never thought I would say that.

Only in the latter stages does the road hug the coast and the views are pleasant rather than spectacular. There have clearly been some Welsh influences in the area as you pass through both Pontypool and

Swansea before you reach a large lagoon area which is the entrance to the Freycinet peninsula where 'pleasant' soon transforms into 'spectacular' and more.

This is meant to be a book about whisky and golf in Tasmania so why am I heading for Freycinet which has no whisky distillery and just a small nine-hole golf course? The golf course was created in 1994 and is attractive and worth playing but is not one you would travel especially to play. I walked around it rather than played it – the condition was good and there were some testing holes as the turf was bouncy and some of the fairways quite narrow. From the top end of the course there were some good views though the course is slightly inland. But Freycinet National Park is certainly somewhere you would travel to – it is extraordinarily beautiful and whatever your plans in Tasmania you should certainly visit here.

It is not a large area and tourist facilities are necessarily limited – there are some nice hotels but not that many. The main settlement is Coles Bay which has a relaxed feel to it, a large beach and delightful coastal paths. There is one road in and out and one main car park. If there is one place you should go, it is to walk up into the hills and take in the view of Wineglass Bay – it is unforgettable. For the more adventurous there are many longer walks in the National Park from a few hours to several days. I was lucky to enjoy a day of sunshine and a cloudless sky with the sea the deepest blue I have ever witnessed and the distinctive terracotta-coloured rocks giving the feel of being somewhere very special. I make no apology for this effusive travelogue – Freycinet is a very special place.

It is a pleasant half-hour drive north to Bicheno, where we come to Waubs Harbour Distillery. I was visiting Waubs Harbour because Rizk at Callington Mill recommended that I should do so and had sent a letter of introduction. This demonstrates the cooperative values of the Tasmanian Whisky industry. Rizk was an enthusiastic and passionate advocate for Callington Mill but was also proud of other entrepreneurial start-ups in Tasmania and was keen that I should experience these as well.

Waubs Harbour is a family business founded by brothers Tim and Rob Polmear and Tim's wife Bec. As ever, there are connections with the heart of the island's industry; Rob had been Head of Production at Lark and Head Distiller at Overeem. But the brothers decided that they would look to create something themselves and the first thing they wanted to do differently was location. They wanted, perhaps inspired by the coastal locations of many of the famous Islay malt distilleries, to create a 'Maritime Tasmanian Single Malt' and so searched for a site on the coast to build their distillery. This brought them to Bicheno on Tasmania's beautiful east coast. Waubs Harbour was the original name of the old fishing village which became the small town of Bicheno. It was thus named after a local aboriginal, Wauba Debar, who became known as 'heroine of the sea' when she rescued two sailors during a storm. Her gravestone can still be visited just along from the distillery.

In some ways I am reminded of Myken, that extraordinary distillery on the small island thirty miles off the coast inside the Arctic Circle in Norway. There the distillery had been built in an old fish-processing factory and here again a new industry is replacing an old one. When they started the Waubs Harbour distillery in 2018, they converted an old oyster catchery in the harbour on the north side of the town. In 2022 they were able to acquire some neighbouring buildings for their expansion plans; these had been an abalone farm so, again, whisky distilling is replacing the declining fishing industry, though Bicheno remains famous for its seafood to this day. The site of the distillery is every bit as scenic as the best that

Islay can offer be it Bowmore, Ardbeg or Bunnahabhain. It is right on the seashore in the harbour overlooking rugged rocks teeming with birdlife. I have always said that location is an essential part of the character of any malt whisky brand – I only like drinking malts from distilleries where I have visited, as the memory of the location and its surroundings somehow contributes to the enjoyment of the dram. If this was the thinking of Rob, Tim and Bec then they got their business off to a great start as it is a very beautiful spot.

Their website clearly states their ambition to create *"a truly maritime Tasmanian single malt whisky that not only embraces but encourages the influence of our wild, coastal provenance, made meticulously and with intention to be rich, oily and distinctively our own."* I am always interested in how start-ups look to define their

**Waubs Harbour's Founder's Reserve
from its 'ocean-cooled distillery'**

own distinctive market position. While location is a good start point, what is critical with whisky is producing a distinctive, high quality, product. Here Rob's experience at Lark and Overeem stands them in good stead. They make their own wash (a number of small Tasmanian distillers will buy in from a brewery) and are wedded to local ingredients: Tasmanian barley and water from the local Apsley river, while they are excited to be experimenting with local peat. This whisky is certainly going to be distinctive as the peat is derived from coastal reeds, melaluca trees and salt bushes. Rob has a background in microbiology and is experimenting with yeasts which can have a significant effect on the nature of the distillate.

And then there is the maturation and the need for quality casks but in looking for distinctiveness the relatively equable coastal climate without any extremes of frost or heat is ideal for their purposes. I remember my first visit to Bunnahabhain as a whisky novice on the shores of the sound of Jura and being told how maturation in the warehouses by the sea gave their whisky a distinctive 'salty' characteristic. I was at the time sceptical but I am now a believer; sea air is different to inland air and casks breathe – so maturing in coastal warehousing is definitely distinctive. Again, I am reminded of the German Distillery, Slyrs in the Bavarian Alps, distilling some of their product on a small boat in the harbour of the small town of List on the northern most point of the island of Sylt in the North Sea. This is what is so wonderful about whisky. What other industry would do such things? Most would be run by accountants who would determine the most cost-effective way of storing product, probably in some massive warehouse centrally located just off a fume-laden motorway junction. But with single malt whisky, location really does mean something. How much real effect does it have on the product? Who knows? But that doesn't matter. Waubs Harbour will be a genuinely 'maritime' whisky because of its location, its use of local ingredients, its special peat and its coastal maturation environment. The end product will be the end product, an undefinable mixture of all these elements. You are buying a product but also a story and as long as it's a good product that is what is important.

Callington Mill and Waubs Harbour are very different but both are symbols of the vibrancy of the Tasmanian whisky industry. The former is a start-up but has had large sums of investment capital behind it. It has set out to be a scale operator and a benchmark for leadership in the industry. Waubs Harbour is a smaller operator which is creating its own distinctive niche. The existence of both is the sign of a healthy industry.

The glorious beach at Barnbougle

Late afternoon sun on the 9th green at Barnbougle Dunes

CHAPTER 4

BARNBOUGLE

I THINK MANY golf enthusiasts will have heard of Barnbougle. Towards the end of the last century, there was a seismic change in the philosophy of golf-course design and a recognition of the unique qualities of links golf. Since the end of WW2 most new courses have been built inland, many in my opinion on unsuitable soil, but from the late 1980s onwards there have been many new courses built on 'links' or at least on sandy and seaside land all around the world. The debate as to what constitutes a 'true links' course has been well rehearsed elsewhere; my simple view is that what matters is the outcome, namely a course that plays like a links with the ball bouncing and running as opposed to soft turf where the ball stops and the game becomes 'target' golf. Arguably the trend started in Ireland where from the late 1980s onwards a number of new links courses were created by the likes of Pat Ruddy, Eddie Hackett and American designers such as Tom Fazio and Gil Hanse (the European Club, Carne, Ballyliffen Glashedy and Rosapenna Sandy Hills). Arguably Arnold Palmer set the tone with the strikingly beautiful Tralee. Kingsbarns was the first big one in Scotland designed by Kyle Phillips in 2000 and others followed there: Castle Stuart, Machrihanish Dunes, Dundonald, Trump International and Dumbarnie. But this was not just an Irish and Scottish phenomenon; 'new classic links' courses began to sprout all over the world with the quality of the site, not its geographic proximity to a golfing market, being the key criterion. Bandon Dunes opened in remote Oregon, Cabot Links in Nova Scotia, Budersand on the island of Sylt in the North Sea. Barnbougle was very much part of this trend. Tasmania, despite Ratho Farm, was not a well-known golfing destination but what was important was the site – links turf and magnificent dunes in a beautiful location, perfect terrain for golf courses.

Time to mention Greg Ramsay again as he is generally credited with being the inspiration behind Barnbougle. Ramsay had spent time in St Andrews in Scotland and recognised the area of links and duneland near the coastal town of Bridport on Tasmania's north-west coast as being a perfect site for building a golf course. The timeline suggests that the opening of Kingsbarns near St Andrews in 2000 may have been a catalyst for his vison – he later became involved in the opening of the new whisky distillery at Kingsbarns. But recognising the quality of the site and having the vison is one thing; realising that vision was another. He needed to do three things: persuade the owner of the land (a local farmer called Richard Sattler who didn't play golf) of the merits of the project; find a group of investors to support the project; and finally persuade a top architect to design a new course on the land. He managed all three with Tom Doak (who had recently completed the highly acclaimed Pacific Dunes, the second course at Bandon Dunes in Oregon) and Mike Clayton working together on the course design. Barnbougle Dunes opened in 2004 and almost immediately became recognised as the best links course in the southern hemisphere.

Such was the success, that Sattler almost immediately began plans for a second course on slightly different land a couple of kilometres along the coast to the east. This time he worked with Chicago entrepreneur Mike Keiser, the major investor behind Bandon Dunes, to create Barnbougle Lost Farm, with the course designed by Bill Coore and Ben Crenshaw, whose most famous creation at the time was probably Sand Hills in Nebraska. As I will describe, it is a slightly different style of course, dictated by the land available, and it is now home to a restaurant and spa as well as more 'premium' style accommodation than the rather basic lodges available at Barnbougle Dunes. More recently, Sattler decided he wanted a short 'fun' course to complement the two big courses and persuaded Bill Coore to design a course on a piece of land he discovered during a bush fire in 2019. Called 'Bougle Run' this is a rather eccentric fourteen-hole course of 12 Par 3s and two Par 4s. Again, more later.

I first visited Barnbougle shortly before Christmas in 2013, less than ten years after the creation of Dunes and just three years after Lost Farm opened. What I liked about it was its lack of exclusivity. It didn't have the air of a high-end resort. Here were two high-quality golf courses, designed by two top designers, and they were open for a reasonable price to anyone. The accommodation was unashamedly 'mid-market' – the new development at Lost Farm perhaps a little smarter than the lodges at the Dunes but the purpose of the 'golf resort' was to come and play two great golf courses. In many ways, ten years on, that is the same. It is not a cheap place to visit but it is not competing in the 'super-premium' sector which is making so many new golf developments outside the reach of the ordinary golfer. We will see this trend in New Zealand. In fact, some of the original 'Lodge' accommodation after twenty years is showing its age (it's described as 3.5 star accommodation) and while new villas have been built, their purpose is clearly to provide accommodation for golfers. Any accompanying non-golfers have a small Spa at Lost Farm but apart from walking along the magnificent beach there is little else to do. Even eating options are limited. The clubhouse at Barnbougle Dunes provides fairly basic 'bar food' while the restaurant at Lost

Farm is better but hardly a destination for a 'foody'. The 'Sports Bar' downstairs is basically a pizza and burger joint. None of this is a criticism – you go there to play golf and it is definitely worth the journey for that.

I decided to play the new Bougle Run course on my first evening having booked to play Lost Farm on the first day and Barnbougle Dunes on the second. After the longish drive up from Freycinet it was the perfect amount of exercise on a warm evening. The 'course' has been squeezed into a small bit of land between the two nines of the main course at Lost Farm; the first two holes and the last two holes are quite near the clubhouse and then you have to walk up into a stretch of quite high dunes where holes 3-12 lie. Bill Coore claims it was the natural topography of this area that dictated the design – it is quite extreme and so Par 3s make sense. It measures 1,791 metres (about 2,000 yards) for its fourteen holes so it is effectively a Par 3 course; the two Par 4s are only 254 and 303 metres respectively. And six of the Par 3s are under 100 metres and the longest only 140 metres. It was fun to play but I'm not sure I can take it too seriously and I am a golfer who doesn't like to take golf too seriously.

I only played it once and maybe it takes a bit of getting used to. I'm not convinced that there are many great Par 3 holes measuring under a hundred yards (ok, maybe the Postage Stamp at Troon is the exception that proves the rule.) Some of the greens were very small and hazardous which is fair enough on a very short hole but at times I wasn't sure they worked – my notes showed 'silly green at 2nd' so clearly I was hard done by there! The first of the Par 4s (4th) is only 254 metres but has a blind drive. Perhaps the best hole was the second Par 4 (8th) with a risk reward drive from on high – the sensible play was a rescue club short but a driver looked very inviting even though I was never going to reach the green over 300 metres away. Don't get me wrong; there were some good holes but to me they were the ones with a more 'normal' length. The most memorable to me were the 5th, only about 130 yards but steeply uphill to a well protected green, and the 10th, this time steeply downhill, about 140 yards, where you had the option of bouncing it in or risk flying it all the way. These were two good Par 3s which would grace any major course.

It was an enjoyable couple of hours. From the high dunes there are good views over the other courses and the coastline. I'm just not sure it added up to much. I'm not against the innovation of fourteen holes – we will come across more of courses with strange numbers of holes in the rest of this book – and Coore claims it was what the land allowed and his brief was to make whatever the land enabled. But a great links is about more than just using a wedge and hoping you judge the length right. With holes of under a hundred yards you are invariably hitting high – I didn't find many bump and run options which you would get on either shorter second shots on Par 4s or perhaps on longer par 3s. I was left wondering whether there might have been just nine good holes with some longer Par 3s – but then I'm not a golf-course designer.

Barnbougle Lost Farm seems to divide opinion. It perhaps suffers from the inevitable comparison with its neighbour as it is less of an authentic links, the middle stretch of holes from about 7 to 13 lying slightly inland. However, these holes certainly don't feel 'parkland'. While they are not seaside holes, the turf is still how it should be for proper bump and run golf. The highlights are probably mid-way through both the front and back 9s. Hole 3 is a great short Par 4, with a well bunkered fairway and an elevated green. 4 is a delightful downhill Par 3 to a green against the estuary and near the beach. The bunker front left will gobble up anything not hit firmly enough. There is then an extraordinary drive at the 5th; the line is a pole on top of a huge dune to your right if you dare. As a Perranporth member, it amused me, as I'm used to blind shots over poles on the top of dunes. 6 is another difficult Par 3 especially in a strong cross wind. It's a great stretch of holes. As you head slightly inland from the 7th, things calm down a bit though the 8th is a challenging, pleasingly shaped Par 5 before the 9th heads back to the clubhouse. The back 9 opens with three long holes – two Par 5s and a 4 – with the blind drive at the Par 4 11 somewhat fearsome. You return to the dunes by the sea at 13, a narrowing Par 4 to a green below the dunes after which you come to the first of Lost Farm's oddities. 13a is an attractive Par 3 sitting high up in the dunes and is the first 'extra' hole of Lost Farm's 20. The second is 18a which is a less interesting Par 3 which you play as you make your way back from the 18th green to the clubhouse. 14 is a great short Par 4 playing down towards the beach and 15 is a very tough long Par 3 between the beach and the enormous dune on top of which sits the Lost Farm restaurant. The finish, 16-18, is a three-hole loop out towards the beach and back with the 17th a memorable Par 3 up into the dunes.

So why twenty holes? The one other course I can think of with twenty holes is the European Club designed by Pat Ruddy at Brittas Bay in south-east Ireland. I know of a number of courses that have 'spare' holes so can be said to have 19 – Kingston Heath and Hayling come to mind. Having an extra hole is a good idea when course maintenance is being undertaken. 13a at Lost Farm is an excellent Par 3 and it's almost a shame that it is not part of the proper course. 18a is a less interesting hole and can be ignored if you wish. In fact, it feels something of an anti-climax after walking off the proper 18th green.

After my morning round I went into the small town of Bridport for a bite of lunch. My impression was that it was looking more well-heeled than when I first visited. I suspect that Barnbougle attracting more tourists to the area has helped. It is an attractive little town and now seems to have a few cafes and restaurants which I don't remember ten years ago.

The sign to the eccentric 14 hole Bougle Run course

It had been very windy for my morning round and by the afternoon the wind had strengthened. The course was not busy but as the premium for playing two rounds in a day was very modest, I decided to brave the wind and go out again. As I have said, the atmosphere at Barnbougle is very relaxed and the staff all very friendly and helpful. I remember asking what tees they recommended I play off. They asked my handicap for guidance but then said 'if I were you, if the hole is downwind, play off the back tees and if it is into the wind, play off the front tees' which is exactly what I did. How sensible was that? There is often a bit of an obsession with golfers wanting to play off the 'back' tees as if this makes the golf course better. I have heard people say you should play it 'as it was designed'. This is a completely false premise. Courses designed a hundred years ago took into account equipment which was completely different so distances are irrelevant. Most modern courses are designed with multiple tees so that golfers of different lengths and abilities can enjoy the same course. There is no point playing off the back tees if you can't hit most of the Par 4s with two good shots – that is not how the course was designed. With the wind gusting around 40mph, choosing which tee to play off at each hole made perfect sense. Isn't golf meant to be enjoyed?

The wind apart, it was a glorious afternoon. As I was playing the 14th I noticed two players behind me. On closer inspection it looked as if it was just a man playing and a lady was walking round with him. I completed my round, had a fun hit on 18a and then wandered slowly back towards the car park after inspecting the Sports Bar. Just as I was walking up the hill, I heard a voice: '*It's Andrew Brown!*' I turned around and there to my astonishment was Martin , a fellow member of Beaconsfield Golf Club, some 10,000 miles to the northwest. It had been him and his wife Alison who had been behind me, Alison deciding that the wind was a bit too strong for her that afternoon. It really is a small world.

We dined together that evening and organised to join up to play Barnbougle Dunes the following morning – for the record it was Alison who took the honours. Perhaps Martin and I can blame the wind of the previous afternoon playing havoc with our finely tuned swings. They left in the afternoon to do some important research at a vineyard – Alison works in the wine trade – and I decided to rest a little before embarking on a late afternoon of nine holes. The wind had eased a little and the light softened. It was my favourite time for golf – late afternoon on a sunny links.

Barnbougle Dunes is a great classic links. It is organised in two loops of 9; the front 9 to the west of the clubhouse and the back 9 to the east. Perhaps the front 9 is more distinctive as the dunes are a little more pronounced though they are not as high and dramatic as at Lost Farm. The back 9, however, is perhaps more classic old links style. The start is modest with a gentle Par 5 and a flattish inland Par 4, before you head towards the dunes. 3 and 4 are both shortish Par 4s with plenty of peril, the enormous bunker at the 4th, set into the dune on top of which nestles the green, typifying the challenge. 5 and 7 are wonderful Par 3s, 5 requiring a long (200-yard plus) shot downhill but with many options on how to play it depending on wind and bounce, and 7 requiring bravery to hit a solid shot (probably a club more than you first thought) to a green perched precipitously on top of another dune. 8 and 9 are two tough Par 4s back to the clubhouse, the former with a tricky two-tier fairway requiring you to be brave and accurate with your drive to have a chance of making it in two.

The back 9 is a little more open and perhaps there are fewer standout holes though I liked the short Par 4 12th where, despite the open aspect, accuracy is required with both the tee shot and the short second into the green. Again, the 9 finishes with two strong Par 4s, a little shorter than on the front 9 but surprisingly they are Stroke 3 and 2 respectively (for non-golfers this is the supposed difficulty rating of the holes), presumably a reflection of them being straight into the prevailing westerly wind.

You would never tire of playing Barnbougle. I will talk a lot in this book about the context of courses and how the scenery is an important part of the golfing experience. Barnbougle is like being on the west coast of Ireland – except on the west coast of Ireland there are no wallabies sitting around the greens nonchalantly watching you putt. They only add to the experience, to the relaxed feel of Barnbougle. Though perhaps the large black snake I saw just off the 4th tee was a little less designed to make me relax – you don't get those in Ireland either. But the beach views are up there with what you get at Tralee, Ballybunion, Lahinch and Rosapenna. The walk from the 4th green to the 5th tee at Barnbougle Dunes or the views from the 15th Tee at Lost Farm are unforgettable.

And Barnbougle is, I think, important in terms of the development of golf. Outside Great Britain, Ireland and North America it was one of the first new developments of what is a classic links style of golf course. Its remote location perhaps dictated that the business plan was not to make it too exclusive. My concern is that many of the new courses built since and in the making will be more exclusive and less accessible – prices at the likes of Kingsbarns and Trump International have increased dramatically in recent years. I understand that these courses are businesses and if the market can bear the prices they charge that makes some sense. But it is a shame for the game of golf if many enthusiasts are priced out of the game.

I obviously always enjoy discovering whisky and golfing links. When embarking on research for this book I had no idea about the golfing and whisky connections of Bothwell. I remember in Germany the thrill of discovering that my chosen distillery, Slyrs in Bavaria, actually matured some of their whisky on the island of Sylt where I had chosen to visit Budersand as my golfing venue. So, it was a delight to learn that Richard Sattler had decided to celebrate the 20th Anniversary of the opening of Barnbougle by partnering with Hellyers Road Distillery to commission a 20 Year Old Special Edition Barnbougle Whisky. It's a limited-edition (only 405 bottles) single-cask whisky from 2004, matured for eighteen years in ex-Bourbon American oak and then finished for two years in a Fortified Tasmanian Ruby Pinot French Oak cask. You can guess my next destination – a perfect segway into my next chapter.

Cradle Mountain National Park

Hellyers Road has the largest stock of maturing malt in Australia

CHAPTER 5

HELLYERS ROAD

HELLYERS ROAD IS not in fact the nearest whisky distillery to Barnbougle. There are now a number in Northern Tasmania, particularly around Launceston, but the nearest is just forty minutes along the coast from Barnbougle. I want to feature Hellyers Road as it is the oldest continually operating distillery in Tasmania and one of the biggest and therefore plays an important role in the industry, but I would urge any whisky enthusiast to visit the wonderfully named Tam O'Shanter Bay at Lulworth where you will find a whisky distillery at the opposite end of the spectrum from Callington Mill and Hellyers Road – Fannys Bay. This is a truly artisan operation, a small business run by a married couple, Mathew and Julie Cooper from a shed in their garden.

You might be wondering about the names. We have already encountered Bothwell and the River Clyde in central Tasmania, the Hobart suburbs of Cambridge, Richmond and Kingston, Swansea and Pontypool on the east coast, so driving from Bridport (which naturally is part of Dorset Council) to Lulworth is not a surprise – you can actually visit Weymouth on the way. The names of Tam O'Shanter and Fannys Bay have a different provenance and relate to a different side of the history of Tasmania – shipwrecks. Over a thousand vessels have been shipwrecked over the years around Tasmania's rugged coastline and often towns, bays and headlands have been named after them. *Tam O'Shanter* was a ship with an unfortunate history of accidents, having run aground outside Adelaide in 1836. After months of repair, it set sail again the following year only to get into trouble in the treacherous Bass Straits and ended up running ashore in the bay it is now named after. *Fanny* was a cutter which on a trip apparently carrying potatoes from the Tamar to Cape Portland on the most north-easterly tip of Tasmania came to grief in another bay just to the east of Tam O'Shanter in 1844. I visited Lulworth beach and Tam O'Shanter Bay which looked calm and beautiful but it was mid-summer. The wind I had experienced at Barnbougle made me understand how the seas around Tasmania have a bad reputation – the weekly ferry service from Melbourne on the *Spirit of Tasmania* is apparently not recommended for those who can suffer from sea sickness.

Mathew was a diesel mechanic and Julie a hairdresser but they seem to be greatly enjoying their retirement running a small whisky business. They set it up in 2014 so in Tasmanian terms this was one of the earlier new distilleries and they are delighted to receive visitors and share their passion for what they make, and to offer you a couple of interesting drams. Mathew has learned on the job but has strong views on quality, believing in using local barley and a long fermentation as well as sourcing high quality and sometimes unusual casks. He is not in a hurry and not interested in scale. Julie describes herself as 'the artistic director' and was the inspiration behind the distinctive square perfume-like bottle while she hand-finishes each label. Call it 'cottage', 'artisan' or 'a lifestyle business' but to me it reflects the diversity of offerings within the industry and this is healthy. And on a visit, you can be assured of personal attention and a good chat about whisky and the beauty of their surroundings.

Lulworth also offers Tam O'Shanter Golf Club. It was founded over thirty years ago and has since built a pleasant clubhouse which has become an important part of the community. I wasn't able to play but the nine holes looked in good condition and the surroundings were quiet and pretty. And it was a bit cheaper than Barnbougle – $20 a day! Lulworth would make a great whisky and golf trip. Indeed, I was beginning to regret not giving time in my itinerary to play local nine-hole courses. I had already missed out on Oatlands and Freycinet and now Tam O'Shanter looked enticing.

The other reason that Hellyers Road attracted me was that it was near to Wynyard Airport at Burnie which was my route onto King Island where I had read about two new links courses. The distillery is situated a few kilometres inland from the coastal town up the hill along what was once a bush trail carved out by an explorer and cartographer, Henry Hellyer, in 1827. The distillery was set up in 1999, very early in Tasmanian terms, and unlike some of its competitors has been operating continuously from the same site since then. It was set up as an offshoot of a dairy cooperative, Betta Milk, now owned by Saputo, a Canadian international dairy company. The distillery is now an independent business though it still shares a site with Saputo and they cooperate closely on services where this is mutually beneficial. Hellyers Road has always been ambitious with its scale and is probably the biggest Tasmanian whisky exporter. I am not sure of the exact timeline of its full independence from Saputo but in 2024 it embarked on a major crowdfunding equity-raising which raised around $4 million Australian from over one thousand investors. The equity raising proposition was centred around a stock of aged whisky valued at $49 million Australian. With their 5,700 casks of aged single malt they claim to own 90% of all Australia's stock of eighteen-year-plus-aged single-malt whisky. This sounds extraordinary but given the relative youth of the industry and Hellyers Road's scale and maturation policy, it is understandable and clearly will put them in a good position for the future. One of the challenges of a cash-hungry whisky start-up is to take the longer-term view and lay down stock to mature, and a number of the Tasmanian businesses didn't or weren't able to take this approach. Perhaps in the early years the dairy business was able to generate cash and so this rather strange food-and-drink pairing made good business sense.

The newly designed Hellyers Road range

The site itself isn't particularly attractive though the view inland from the back of the site towards the mountains and further up 'Hellyers Road' is pretty. There is a professional 'Cellar Door' experience and a high-quality café where I enjoyed lunch before being shown around by their Brand Manager, Kit Wilkinson. Again, I had been introduced by Rizk who had emailed their Chairman Lesley French and CEO Derek Charge. Kit is an Englishman who worked for UK retailers before emigrating to Tasmania and was clearly enjoying working for the business. Despite its fairly remote location it is currently the most visited whisky distillery in Tasmania though perhaps Callington Mill and the new Lark site might challenge that in the future. One feature of the tour is the chance to fill, seal and label your own bottle of whisky – a nice touch.

Inside, it is more like visiting a food factory than a distillery. There is a lot of stainless steel and no feature still house with quaint copper pot stills. The pots of the stills are stainless steel while the heads, necks and lyne arms are made of copper. They are, in relative terms, run very slowly to maximise reflux. The mash-tun is also not conventional as it sists on its side which apparently makes cleaning easier. The site also included maturation warehousing and even a cooperage.

I visited a few months before the equity raising but it was clear that the business was in a growth phase. They were undertaking a major rebranding. The old bottle was a rather slim, 'un-whisky-like' wine bottle and the design a drawing depicting Henry Hellyer on his 'road'. It was quaint and distinctive but perhaps not what was required for their growth ambitions particularly in export. This design was being replaced with a more classic whisky-shaped bottle and premium design with the brand Hellyers Road supported by 'North West Tasmania' clearly an attempt to differentiate themselves from the major brands in the south of the state. It will also aid communication of many different expressions – a requirement of any growth strategy.

I noticed that shortly after my visit Kit's role changed to become 'Shareholder Relationship Manager' reflecting the new business structure. Hellyers Road is an unusual business in that it emerged out of a dairy cooperative – perhaps surprising that dairy farmers should decide to invest in a whisky distillery. Now it is a focused whisky business and its history is something of a strength as it has not been subject to some of the corporate shenanigans that characterise the history of the likes of Lark, Overeem and even Sullivan's Cove. Corporate changes are a feature of any growing industry – we have seen many similar confusing ownership changes in the Scotch whisky industry – but often those businesses which have enjoyed corporate stability do best in the long term. William Grant, owners of Glenfiddich, which I featured in my last Scottish book, are a great example.

Having visited five Tasmanian whisky distilleries, it is perhaps time to reflect on the industry though with my five visits I have only really touched the surface. The consensus seems to be that there were now between seventy and eighty operating distilleries in Tasmania. And let me remind you of some facts: Tasmania's population is around 600,000 and that's less than the population of Glasgow. It is remarkable. The whisky industry in other countries has also shown that there is room for many different types of operator. This explosion in number of distilleries has taken place in the past ten to fifteen years – there were just eight distilleries operating in 2012.

I don't intend to even try to give a short history of the industry but merely offer some reflections. The industry has had its issues and complications. Lark purchased Overeem and was then acquired by Australian Whisky Holdings which also acquired Nant (probably not a good move) before selling off the Overeem brand back to the family who have regenerated it in a new distillery. The Shene Distillery at Pontville was invested in by a number of industry players and then sold to Australian Whisky Holdings to become the main site for Lark – Australian Whisky Holdings, subsequently rebranding themselves as Lark Distilling. The sale of Pontville then enabled the building of

Callington Mill. Don't try to follow all this – I am just demonstrating that any burgeoning industry will produce complicated corporate relationships. Lark at Pontville, Callington Mill and Hellyers Road will be the scale operators but they all have very different histories and different assets. The Lark operation now has a slightly corporate feel to it but its brand story is enormously strong; Callington Mill is the best invested with a new turnkey site; Hellyers Road has a valuable amount of aged stock. Waubs Harbour will be a small, premium operator with a distinctive approach and should ride with the market growth. Fannys Bay will remain very small and artisan and be very happy being so. Whisky is a market that can accommodate all these types of business. Eighty distilleries feels like an enormous number and there may be some casualties or indeed some industry consolidation but I think the years ahead will be exciting ones and in global terms I believe the awareness and reputation of Tasmanian whisky will begin to take off.

An 'infinity green' at Ocean Dunes on King Island

The magnificent wooden jetty at Naracoopa on
the remote east coast of King Island

CHAPTER 6

KING ISLAND (1)

BEFORE HEADING TO King Island, I took a quick trip up Cradle Mountain. Tasmania has some nineteen national Parks and numerous Conservation Areas. Cradle Mountain is over 1,500 metres high and often visitors are disappointed as there are many days when it is shrouded in cloud. I was lucky, arriving late afternoon and enjoying a walk in the sunshine and meeting a grazing wombat on my way to view the waterfalls at Pencil Pine Creek. The landscape reminded me of the Cairngorms and I enjoyed my very brief visit.

Cradle Mountain has an important part to play in the story of the rebirth of Tasmanian Whisky as the forerunner to the current Cradle Mountain Whisky company arguably pre-dates Lark. In 1989 Brian Poke received a licence to undertake experimental trials to make whisky out of a Tasmanian variety of barley called Franklin. Initially this was under the Darwin Distillery name, Darwin being the location of the laboratory where the initial tests took place. But the first distillation took place in Tasmania in 1989 – the year of Bill Lark's fishing trip – and over subsequent years the distillery was moved to various locations in north-west Tasmania and was renamed Franklin Distillery. Various ownership and name-changes followed until 2015 when the distillery was sold and rebranded Cradle Mountain Whisky with a new distillery site in the Tamar Valley Region. You will only find Cradle Mountain Whisky in the bars of the Cradle Mountain hotels so its geographical provenance is a little suspect.

I was heading off the mainland – mainland Tasmania, itself an island off mainland Australia. Australia is technically of course not an island but a 'continental landmass' though looks quite like a very big island to me. King Island is one of many significant islands off Tasmania; Flinders Island off the north-east coast, Maria Island off the east coast and Bruny Island south of Hobart are all worth visiting. King Island, off the north-west coast is the second largest. It is just over sixty kilometres long and just under thirty wide. It's just a little larger than the Isle of Mull but with a much smaller population of about 1,600. Getting there is not easy – it is located in the middle of the Bass Straits and only has a weekly freight ferry service from Melbourne. For passengers the only option is to fly, and three small airlines go there from Melbourne, Hobart, Launceston and Wynyard Airport at Burnie which was where I had booked from.

My journey was not quite what I expected. The aircraft are not 747s or Dreamliners. Mine was a 17-seater operated by Sharp Airlines which I had booked some six months previously in order to fit in with my schedule. It was a pleasant Sunday morning as I drove down from Cradle Mountain towards the coast. I had to drop off my hire car so arrived at the airport and, as I was in unfamiliar territory, I had left plenty of time and arrived about an hour and a half before the flight. There was no one at the car hire drop off just across the road but I posted the keys through a letterbox and wheeled my luggage across to the airport. I walked up to the terminal building which looked quiet. And it was quiet. Very quiet! The door was locked – no one about. I checked my ticket – had I got the wrong time or even the wrong day? All seemed in order – I had even checked in online. I walked around the perimeter of the airport – no signs of anything, not one aeroplane. Hmm.

I had been getting increasingly anxious when about forty-five minutes before the take-off time a car drew up and parked in the car park. A woman got out and approached the front of the airport. She had a business-like air about her and produced a set of keys from her pocket, opened the door and turned on the lights. She seemed unsurprised that I had been waiting. Over the next forty-five minutes she manned the check-in desk (other passengers did arrive about half an hour before the flight) undertook the baggage security check, drove the baggage cart to the aircraft (which had just arrived), loaded the baggage onto the aircraft and then donned a pair of headphones to undertake air traffic control duties. This was impressive multi-skilling. There was a moment when I thought she might also pilot the plane.

I was in Seat 1A with my right knee pretty close to the pilot's left shoulder. It was a glorious day with not a cloud in sight and the forty-minute flight was delightful, the deep blue of the sea competing with the bright blue of the cloudless sky. King Island Airport was small but smart and very efficient. My car-hire company (two local companies serve the island, no Hertz or Avis there) was there to meet me and told me on return to park the car opposite the terminal and leave the keys in the ignition. They clearly enjoy telling tourists to do this though when you discover that your car is a rather battered old Peugeot with 235,000 kilometres on the clock you are a little less surprised! Indeed, who is going to steal a car on such a small island with no way of getting it to the mainland?

Historically, King Island's economy was largely agricultural, it being famous for cheese, beef, seafood and kelp. All these survive today. An old tungsten mine operated for nearly a century but this closed when prices were depressed in the 1990s. However, growing demand has seen it recently re-open which can only boost the island's fragile economy. The building of two top-class golf courses was part of a plan to develop tourism with golf, seen as a premium niche which could attract limited numbers of high-value customers. I had read about these two new courses and decided that they merited a visit.

Heidi's small still at the King Island Distillery

First, however, I headed straight for the King Island Golf and Bowling Club in the main town, Currie, which describes itself as 'the Home of Links Golf on King Island.' Indeed until a few years ago the course, which dates back to 1938, was the only golf on King Island. The old clubhouse sits in an elevated position overlooking the coast. There is a touch of faded grandeur (perhaps more faded than grand) about the building but there was a bustle of activity (possibly more bowlers than golfers) and a warm welcome when I asked if I could buy a green fee and hire some clubs.

The barman took my green fee and suggested that I just helped myself to any of the bags of clubs which were stacked in the doorway as nobody seemed to have decided on a hire fee. A couple of lady golfers were just teeing off and I was happy to follow them.

The course needs some explanation; it's not really a nine-hole course as there are seventeen different tees and twelve greens. 9 and 18 are completely different holes while 5 and 14 and 6 and 15 play to different greens (along the same fairway) on the back 9 (though 5 and 14 have the same tee.) Are you following me? Don't worry, just embrace it and enjoy it. This is fun golf with hard bounces, changes in elevation and wind always a factor.

The location is scenic with lovely views across the coastline. The holes make their way down to and along the coast and then back up the hill to the clubhouse. The best holes are probably those at the beginning and end of the two nines which use the hill. It was late January in high summer and the course was very burnt and hard. In truth it was not in good condition but it tested your game and your control of the ball. The turf is rather variable with the sea clearly impacting it in places. But there are some memorable holes, perhaps the best being the Par 3 $3^{rd}/12^{th}$ where the tees are high up, facing the ocean and the green down below just above the beach. I had no idea what club to take: about 160 yards but dramatically downhill yet into a strong wind. This is the type of golf I like: no mechanical calculations, just feel. I ended up at the back of the green and was happy.

The middle three seaside holes are perhaps less interesting but 7,8 and 9 all use the steep slope to create challenging holes. 7 plays downhill across shrubland while 8 plays sharply uphill to a green attractively situated by some trees. 9 is a short Par 4 to a gathering green and 18 a Par 3 played straight uphill to a plateau immediately in front of the clubhouse. It's around 170 yards but required a good smack and I was relieved to see my ball cling onto the edge of the green. It's not great golf but it was certainly fun golf.

The King Island Golf and Bowling Club now also hosts an independently run excellent restaurant. This is much needed in Currie because there is little else. I could mention 'The Boathouse' in Currie Harbour which advertises itself as 'the restaurant with no food'. You get a table and settings but bring your own food and drink. This is the challenge for King Island – there is a lack of quality accommodation and restaurants to cater for the golfing tourist. If, as I go on to describe, my golfing experience was spectacularly good, my accommodation in Currie was spectacularly bad but I will spare you the details. If tourism is going to be an important part of the island's economy there is going to need to be investment in both accommodation and dining options. The island has about 130 beds for tourists – indeed it has been said that there are more bunkers than beds on the island.

Outside of Currie there are only two small settlements of note: Narracoopa with its long wooden pier on the almost deserted east coast and Grassy in the south where the tungsten mine is situated. Currie Harbour is attractive and you can drive the 'kelp road' along the coast past the golf course and visit the small museum in the old lightkeeper's house. That apart there is not a great deal for the tourist to do.

It was perhaps wrong of me to reflect on the Tasmanian whisky industry in the last chapter before coming here as King Island has a distillery. In fairness, it is not a focused whisky distillery as it produces a range of products: gins, moonshine, vodka and even limoncello! It is run by 'happy' Heidi Weitjens, as she describes herself, and she is certainly an enthusiast not just for her distillery but for all things on

King Island. She is from a dairy farming family and grew up on the island and is a well-known local personality. As you will understand with a population of around 1,600 most people know most people. As well as running her small distillery she is President of the island's Chamber of Commerce and even spent some time as the temporary editor of the island's newspaper.

This is an artisan operation located in a green shed just off the racecourse which is one of Currie's main landmarks. The distillery makes Fannys Bay look like a high-tec automated operation. It's the first distillery visit I have had when I was accompanied by a dog – I have a photograph to prove it. But as well as being a local personality Heidi is well known within the Tasmanian industry for her infectious positivity – again Rizk had given me an introduction. We chatted about all things whisky and she insisted that I tasted her latest innovation – a brandy matured in a whisky cask. 'Why not?' she said. Why not indeed. Her business relies heavily I think on the island's tourism and, as we will see, with this likely to increase, she certainly has something to build on. One thing you can rely on with Heidi is that a distillery visit will be fun.

The view over the 18th hole to the famous lighthouse at Cape Wickham

**The sound of the sea is a constant background
to playing at Cape Wickham**

CHAPTER 7

KING ISLAND (2)

THE REASON I had come to King Island was to play two new links courses which I had read about. Tasmania has so much to see and so much variety that it is difficult for King Island to get itself added to a tourist itinerary. In fact, someone wanting to add an island to a visit to Tasmania would probably go to the slightly bigger but even less populated Flinders Island. Topographically, Flinders Island is more varied with mountains and a National Park while King Island is essentially flat. Flinders Island also has a whisky distillery, Furneaux Distillery, which is a more whisky-focused farm operation. It is well known for its beaches, its seafood and it attracts many walkers.

This is where golf plays such an important role on King Island. My marketing background would always make me approach the challenge of King Island wanting to attract more visitors by looking for differentiation. It probably can't compete with Flinders Island on the beauty of its landscape and it is not going to be any easier or cheaper to get there. What it does have is a magnificent coastline and an established old golf course. So, to build new links golf courses to attract 'premium' tourists makes perfect sense. I don't know exactly how it happened but, with hindsight, it seems obvious. And I can tell you they have started in the right way. Any marketer will also tell you that if you are going to invest in a product it needs to be top quality. I am pleased to report that the courses do not disappoint. And the plan is working with tourist numbers trebling over the past ten years to a level of around 18,000 per year. Investment in accommodation will need to follow soon.

I will start with Ocean Dunes, which is situated on the west coast just north of Currie so very accessible from the main centre of population, such that it is. 'Ocean' and 'Dunes' describes the course and the setting perfectly as it is set in a magnificent area of duneland right by the ocean.

Ocean Dunes is now owned by a Melbourne consortium but the architect was Graeme Grant who had been for many years the supervisor at Kingston Heath so you can imagine the type of golf here. There are two loops of nine with six of the holes (1-4 and 10 and 11) hugging the ocean while the other holes play into the dunes so you have a combination of low-level coastal vistas with crashing waves and higher viewpoints from greens looking down towards the sea. It is a delight. There is every type of hole: sweeping Par 5s (1st), tricky short Par 4s (2nd), tough long Par 4s (3, 9 and 18) and four characterful Par 3s. Which holes to mention? The Par 3 10th playing across the bay below the clubhouse is an obvious choice though the Par 3 4th is as good. I also enjoyed the slightly inland stretch from 12-15, holes of character with shape and big elevation changes. Perhaps if there is a disappointment, it is 9 and 18, the finish of each 9 which are both good holes but each of the greens are hidden away from the rest of the course so on putting out you don't get a feeling of where you are.

The current clubhouse is small and modest. When I was there, I was told about plans for new accommodation at Ocean Dunes and I have learned since that a $35 million Australian investment has been agreed together with a loan from the Tasmanian Government to build a sixty-four-room hotel with restaurant and bar. This is tremendous news for the whole island. I haven't seen the plans but if the new buildings can be somewhere near the 9th and 18th greens this will help the make-up of the site and the sixty-four rooms will add a much needed 50% to the amount of tourist accommodation available on the island.

**Best not to try and find your ball in the
deep rough at Cape Wickham!**

Golf buggies are called 'golf carts' in Australia and New Zealand. Incidentally golf 'trolleys' are called 'trundlers', a term, with a hint of onomatopoeia, which I rather like and think we should adopt in the U.K. It is perhaps surprising that in my four books I have not addressed the issue of buggies, trollies and the like. You will perhaps not be surprised to learn that generally I am not a fan of buggies. For me the walking of a golf course is part of the game and I particularly dislike some of the new courses which are designed specifically for buggies. I use a trolley these days (and have even in recent years resorted to an electric one) as my back can hurt from carrying but I actually prefer to carry so that I can walk exactly where I want. I also find buggies sometimes rather anti-social while they can actually slow play down when two people who are sharing drive to different parts of the fairway. They also seem to interrupt the rhythm of golf as rounds can slow down then suddenly speed up.

I have, however, moderated my views on golf buggies in recent years for two reasons. First, if someone can only manage to carry on playing golf by using a golf buggy then surely they should be encouraged. I know a few people like this and it is wonderful that they can still play. The design of smaller, single buggies is helping with this. Secondly, I have discovered another occasion when taking a buggy makes sense. I was on King Island for two days and wanted to play both Ocean Dunes and Cape Wickham twice – thirty-six holes a day. They are big courses and big walks. At Ocean Dunes in particular there are some long walks between holes – on some courses I would criticise this but here I can understand it as they had plenty of land to play with. I used a buggy on both days and as well as making my 36 holes on two consecutive days manageable, it allowed me on courses with which I was not familiar, to explore the holes a little before playing them. On neither day were the courses busy; I was playing on my own. I could go to my ball and then drive ahead to understand what lay in front of me – particularly useful on blind and semi-blind shots. I don't use GPS devices and rely simply on 150-yard markers or their equivalent. But I rely most of all on feel and what I see. Having a buggy to go ahead and see the land before playing the shot was very helpful on both courses. I repeated this on a couple of the new courses I played in New Zealand. One word of warning about taking a buggy on Ocean Dunes; the track from the clubhouse down to the 10th tee is steeply downhill and somewhat precipitous. It would not be advised after too many whiskies.

A magazine called *Australian Golf Digest* published its rankings for the best hundred golf courses in Australia in 2024 and caused something of a stir. For many years Royal Melbourne and Kingston Heath, those two gems on Melbourne's famous sand belt, had been ranked numbers one and two. In 2024, Cape Wickham on King Island was given the top spot. So, is this justified or is this just part of the hype of a new links built in a spectacular location?

Cape Wickham is about a forty-minute drive to the north on the only road up the island, misleadingly called the B25 – there are certainly not twenty-five roads on King Island. As you are approaching the northern tip of the island, the road changes to a dirt track which proved a bit of a challenge for my rather ancient battered Peugeot which began to rattle even more noisily. You pass the iconic lighthouse and then come across a rather disappointing looking portacabin which is the clubhouse and restaurant for Cape Wickham Golf Links. It is the only disappointing thing there is. There are sixteen chalets tastefully designed sitting on top of the dunes. The site was developed by an Australian businessman who commissioned the American architect Mike DeVries to design the course. More recently it has been sold to a Vietnamese investor. The chalet accommodation is excellent though not luxurious (don't expect much in the way of Wi-Fi), and the restaurant, based in the fairly basic portacabin, offered some top-class food.

What a view! I arrived in the evening but the location and the look of the course whetted my appetite for the following day. I slept well to a chorus of wild animals and birds and the constant sound of the sea. Meeting a copperhead snake sitting outside my chalet door did momentarily shake me and served to ensure I took seriously the warnings not to go into the deep rough. The wallabies and wild turkeys which I also met on the course were more engaging.

The layout is different from Ocean Dunes – there are thirteen holes south of the clubhouse and then five finishing holes loop around north up to the lighthouse and back. There are 8 ocean hugging holes where the splash of the waves on the rocky coastline is a constant companion. There are so many other great holes. The first tee shot from up on high to a fairway which looks tiny but is actually a reasonable width sets the tone. It screams peril but just requires a confidently hit shot although with the wind howling off the sea this is easier said than done. Every hole is a highlight but maybe the highlights of the highlights are the seaside holes 10, 11 and 12 and then 17 and 18. 10 plays strongly downhill to a green by the sea, 11 is a lovely Par 3 across the coast line and 12 a tight dogleg short Par 4 which again hugs the coast. 17 is probably the best of the Par 3s again along the coast and then 18 a long par 4 with a risk and reward drive angled across the beach. In this respect with such a memorable finish it has the edge over Ocean Dunes. And everywhere, everywhere there are the views, the glorious, magnificent, wonderful views. I quickly ran out of adjectives to describe them.

Golf course rankings are, as I have said before, ultimately a matter of opinion – or a sum of different opinions. Is Cape Wickham really 'better' than Royal Melbourne? I have read some critical reviews of Cape Wickham – one rather pompous one from 'a + handicap golfer' (I think he wanted us to know his credentials) gave a critique of each hole summarising many of them as 'bad design' or 'poor design' and complained at the end of the '9 blind shots'. I don't think I will invite him to Perranporth or St Enodoc! Let's just say that I couldn't disagree more.

It is a great golf course – I can't think of a criticism or a weak hole. It is Kingsbarns but more dramatic. It is Pebble Beach without the rather bland inland holes. It is Dornoch but possibly even better. It is perfectly structured with two Par 3s and two Par 5s on each 9 which is how it should be. There are different tee lengths for different standards of golfer. The holes go in every possible direction so judging the wind is a real art. The sea is sometimes to your right and sometimes to your left. The quality of the grass is good, the greens are firm and the bunkering is strategic. You need to think and you need to play lots of different shots – this is running golf, not target golf. And you finish on 18 with that magnificent long Par 4 played across and then alongside the beach (which, as at Machrihanish, North Berwick and Dornoch, is an integral part of the course) to a green sitting below the clubhouse. It's a great hole. On my second round I parred it – I can't tell you what a thrill that was.

Am I influenced by the location? Yes, I am happy to acknowledge that because I believe that location is part of the golfing experience. Did the spectacular views and the lovely weather colour my judgement on the innate quality of the course? I don't think so – I will talk about a course in New Zealand with equivalent views but where I have some design criticisms. I also think that you can overplay the role of 'design' – put it this way, there is quite a big grey area between a 'well' designed hole and a 'badly' designed hole. To me what is important is the golfing experience over eighteen holes; the quality of the turf, the layout, the changes in elevation and direction, the mix and variety of holes, the ability to play bump and run shots as well as fully flighted ones and the environment around you as you face the test. Cape Wickham delivers handsomely on all these.

The following week I played Royal Melbourne. It is an extraordinary golf course. A wonderful place. It was a privilege to play it. But Royal Melbourne is situated in a Melbourne suburb and the two courses are spread over four different patches of land called 'paddocks'. For the West Course you play on two of these and on the East you play on three. This means you have to cross streets of traffic. There are traffic lights. For me this affects the experience. The course is pretty but there are no wider views. There is traffic noise. You feel that you are in a city; you are in a city.

Cape Wickham couldn't be more different. Its remoteness is part of its appeal. If you want that '*Joy to be alive feeling*' as coined by Lorne Smith in his *Fine Golf* website then Cape Wickham will deliver just that. I have often been asked what my favourite golf course in the world is and I have usually mumbled that I couldn't choose just one but if I had to come up with a short list it might include Machrihanish, Dornoch and Brora and possibly Cruden Bay – but after my memorable twenty-four hours there, I think Cape Wickham might be even better than those.

The wonderful 18th green at Royal Melbourne

The New South Wales Club has wonderful views over Botany Bay

CHAPTER 8

MAINLAND INTERMISSION

MELBOURNE AND SYDNEY

I HAVE DELIBERATELY chosen to focus this book on Tasmania because of its very distinct contribution to the Australian whisky industry. After all, a state with just over 2% of the country's population has at least 33% of the country's whisky distilleries. There is of course still a lot happening elsewhere in Australia from small malt whisky start-ups to large-scale grain distillery operations. This book is too short to embark on any serious analysis of the Australian whisky industry. Australia's vast territories mean that there are many different 'terroirs' and climates in which these distilleries are operating so it is in any case too early in the industry's development to identify a particular style to Australian whisky. If perhaps there is one notable feature, it is the use of casks from its well-established wine industry. This has led to some criticism from whisky experts that some distilleries have used ex-fortified wine casks as a short-cut to creating flavour, thereby producing full-bodied, strong flavoured but somewhat unsubtle whiskies.

For golf, I knew about Barnbougle and its pioneering role as a forerunner of a trend to build 'new classic' links courses outside of the United Kingdom and Ireland with Cape Wickham and Ocean Dunes being more recent examples. The discovery that Tasmania also boasted Australia's oldest golf course was a bonus. But as I had visited both Melbourne and Sydney, I wanted to say something about a few of the historic golf courses there as they are internationally renowned.

This was my third visit to Australia – they have all been ten years apart; 2004, 2014 and 2024. It's thanks to my youngest sister, Lucy, that I have enjoyed these trips. She has lived in Australia for over thirty years. I flew back from the small King Island Airport to Essendon Airport at Melbourne – this was originally Melbourne's main airport until it was replaced by the nearby Tullamarine in 1970. I was blessed again with a cloudless sky and a wonderful birds-eye view of the enormous Bay of Melbourne from the small seventeen-seater plane. The contrast of the small, sparsely populated King Island and the five million inhabitants of the greater Melbourne area could not have been greater. What it did confirm was the potential market for the King Island golf courses just a short forty-five-minute flight away.

On my second visit in 2014, I had been lucky enough to play golf at both Kingston Heath and the neighbouring Yarra Yarra on the Melbourne sand belt. Yarra Yarra had an informal reciprocal arrangement with my club, Beaconsfield, while Lucy, through her gardening business, had a client who was a member of Kingston Heath. I was royally treated at both and thoroughly enjoyed the courses with their sandy soil and bouncy, linksy style. I gather that recently Yarra Yarra has been upgraded by Tom Doak's design firm. On this occasion, Lucy, who doesn't know a lot about golf, told me that she had another client who was a member of a 'famous club in Melbourne'. I asked her which one. 'Um, I think it might be Royal something. Is there a Royal Melbourne?' I swallowed and took a deep breath. 'Royal Melbourne? You can get me a game at Royal Melbourne?' 'Oh yes, no problem. We just need to agree a date.'

Lucy had lived for the past twenty years on a small farm on the Murray River some three hours' drive north of Melbourne, just across the border in New South Wales. I had played the local course at Tocumwal (which is actually in Victoria) in 2004 and was delighted to play it again – courtesy of another of Lucy's clients! The club at Tocumwal has three nine-hole loops set amongst the trees and is an excellent test of golf. The climate can be challenging and the fairways are firm and often tight putting a premium on accurate shot-making. The greens are good. There is plenty of variety across the twenty-seven holes so you wouldn't tire of playing here. The soil is sandy along the Murray River so is excellent for golf courses and there are a number of good ones. Perhaps the best is at Yarrawonga, about forty minutes to the east of Tocumwal. It has forty-five holes and is a popular destination for golf trippers from Melbourne.

I played Royal Melbourne on a day when temperatures were forecast to rise into the high 30˚s. I was playing with a member, David, a retired surgeon who lived locally while also owning a holiday home near to my sister in Tocumwal. There was some discussion as to whether to proceed but it would have taken more than a bit of heat to put me off. As it happened, the following day the blistering heat exploded into a massive storm which I watched burst over the city from my hotel at the airport. The whole area flooded badly – golf would certainly not have been possible. Lady luck had again shined on me.

There is an immediate air of opulence as you drive into Royal Melbourne, a feeling of both quality and scale. The large clubhouse is like a five-star hotel with lots of memorabilia and dedications to the course's famous architect, Alister MacKenzie. The club dates back to 1891 and gained its Royal prefix from Victoria in 1895 though the courses we play today were built in the late 1920s. The club had moved from its original site to Sandringham in 1901 but it was the visit of Alastair MacKenzie in 1926 that saw the building of the West Course on neighbouring land at Black Rock where the club now resides. Of course, MacKenzie never saw the fruits of his design; the project, along with the design of the East Course was undertaken by Alex Russell, a club member and winner of the 1924 Australian Open, along with the club greenkeeper, Mick Morcom. The courses were not completed until 1931, some five years after MacKenzie's visit.

In some ways there are three courses at Royal Melbourne: the West, the East and the Composite course which is used for competitions. It is not dissimilar in this respect to Walton Heath or Gullane though at both of these only two holes are used from respectively the New course and Gullane No 2. At Royal Melbourne, the composite course, comprises twelve holes from the West and six from the East. This is because Royal Melbourne's courses are spread across four different pieces of land, the 'paddocks', which are separated by residential streets. Nowadays there are traffic lights to ensure safe passage for golfers. The West Course is spread across two paddocks and the East across three. So, visitors never play the Royal Melbourne used in tournaments and indeed the members themselves seldom do. The courses are very similar in style as the land and turf is all the same.

I played the East and I have to say found the process of crossing roads to different paddocks a little disorientating. I like to be able to remember a course's routing but here I didn't, though I can remember many wonderful individual holes. In this respect, it is a very different experience from the likes of Barnbougle and Cape Wickham where the wider views from the course are constant. The main paddock actually contains twenty-one holes (fourteen on the West and seven on the East) and feels more like a golf course because the paddock is large and also contains the clubhouse so there is a feeling of space. The East's contribution to the Composite course are holes 1 and 2 (played as 3 and 4), holes 3 and 4 (played as 15 and 16) and 17 and 18 which also provide the wonderful finish on the composite.

The golf is strongly 'links-like' with firm fairways and fast greens. The greens are generally large with many undulations and surrounded

**Portrait of Alister MacKenzie in the
Royal Melbourne clubhouse**

by enormous bunkers. Every shot requires thought – often you need to think about where the best 'miss' might be. My main memories of the East are the holes on the main paddock. There are two magnificent Par 3s (4 and 16 – 16 actually is sometimes used instead of 4 on the Composite course), 4 being strongly uphill to an offset green and 16 slightly downhill to a trickily shaped green surrounded by bunkers. Having said that, all the greens at Royal Melbourne are surrounded by bunkers. 17 and 18 are also great holes; 17 is a Par 5 of some 570 yards and while the drive at the sweeping Par 4 18 looks inviting with a huge wide fairway, where you end up will very much dictate the difficulty of your second. The test of a great golf course is whether playing it week in and week out, you will continue to be challenged. That will certainly be the case at Royal Melbourne and members have two such courses – what a privilege it must be to be a member here.

My host at Tocumwal was an Englishman, a Sydney-based lawyer, who had a holiday home in Tocumwal. When he learned that I was spending a few days in Sydney on the way back from New Zealand, he invited me to Royal Sydney. It really does pay to have a sister with good contacts! Peter was very apologetic because the golf course at Royal Sydney was at the time closed for a major overhaul – and when I say 'major overhaul' I mean it, as the famous old course was closed for a period of fifteen months while Gil Hanse built what in effect was a completely new golf course on the same land.

Peter kindly introduced me to many of the management team at the club as well as a number of members and I was able to talk through both the history and the future. The Royal Sydney Golf Club is more than a just golf club; it is an institution with, as well as an eighteen- and a nine-hole golf course, eighteen tennis courts, two bowling greens, two croquet lawns, two squash courts and a Fitness Centre. This is not to mention the billiard tables which its elegant clubhouse is famous for. The clubhouse also contains some magnificent golfing memorabilia. The club, like Royal Melbourne, dates from the 1890s and was granted its Royal prefix in 1897 but unlike Royal Melbourne has occupied the same Rose Bay site throughout its history. It's just a fifteen-minute ferry ride from Circular Quay in the centre of Sydney to the Rose Bay terminal and then a short five-minute walk to the club and the golf course occupies the hill above overlooking Sydney Harbour. It's a great location.

Changes to golf courses can be controversial. I sometimes ask the question 'why?' I often come across clubs changing this hole and that, moving bunkers, adding bunkers, taking other bunkers away. When this is done in an *ad hoc* fashion, it rarely works.

What Royal Sydney has done is certainly not *ad hoc*. A decision was taken that big changes were needed – tree cover had increased with the resultant lower light levels affecting the turf and causing drainage issues and increased maintenance costs. The course had also tumbled in the rankings from being commonly in the Top 6 to struggling to make the Top 50. What is impressive was the decision to undertake one big project: close the course for eighteen months and design a new course. The new course will be more heathland in style than parkland, with old trees being replaced with, I was told, 2,187 new ones and 500,000 native plants. Sustainability has been a core principle with the new course requiring 20% less water and less fertiliser to maintain it. By starting again Royal Sydney can be created to modern design principles – a golf course should be naturally sympathetic to its landscape. This can also extend to the layout which will be two loops of nine, a 64% increase in fairway space and a more strategic approach to bunker placement. I sensed much excitement amongst both the staff and the members at the prospect of the new course which will be something to be proud of.

At the time of writing the course seems on track to open in March 2025 – I hope that one day I may be able to play it.

I did, however, find time to play one course in Sydney, the New South Wales Golf Club on the La Perouse peninsula overlooking Botany Bay where Captain Cook first sailed into Australia in 1770. The New South Wales was another product of Alister MacKenzie's famous 1826 trip to Australia. The club already existed and MacKenzie produced a layout which was initially built 'unbunkered' with the final layout and bunkering produced by the well-known Australian amateur golfer Eric Appleby, during the 1930s. The course was requisitioned by the army during the war and Appleby returned to restore the course in 1948. There is some debate as to how much of what exists today reflects MacKenzie's exact layout but I'm not sure that is important. While not a 'true links', its undulating clifftop location and sandy soil makes it a perfect site for a golf course with the added advantage over Royal Melbourne of its wonderful views. It is hard to believe that you are only about twenty minutes from the city centre though I suppose Sydney offers plenty of spectacular locations twenty minutes from its centre. This is a tough golf course with hard fairways and slick, often raised, greens on a windy site. I was lulled into a false sense of security by parring the short but tight Par 4 first hole. I took more shots, however, to complete the long Par 3 second! The course then zig-zags its way out to the coast with the three holes, 5-7 being the most commonly photographed. 5 is a long Par 5 with a blind drive over a hill and then down to a green on the coast. 6 is the famous Par 3 across the bay while 7 is a long par 4 which climbs back up the hill away from the coast with the routing returning to the clubhouse at 9. It's an exhilarating part of the course.

The back 9 follows a similar path with the coastal holes this time being higher up, four differing, tricky dog-leg Par 4s before the short

17th and long Par 5 18th return you once again to the safety of the smart clubhouse. I played in a fourball with a young, low-handicap American and an elderly American couple with high handicaps, but the course was hugely enjoyable for all, which in my view is a good test for a great golf course.

It's expensive to play as a visitor and they require a letter of introduction from your club, something that used to be quite common but is less prevalent today. It probably ensures that the visitors they get are wanting to play for the right reasons. The greeting was friendly and the atmosphere relaxed and the green fee included full use of the practice area. Golf is becoming expensive but there are options as we will see in New Zealand where I was to pay some of the most expensive green fees I have ever experienced as well as some of the best value you will find anywhere in the world today.

The tartan clad tasting room at Whisky Galore in Christchurch

The peaceful Botanical Gardens in the centre of Christchurch

CHAPTER 9

CANTERBURY

My first glimpse of New Zealand was from the aeroplane flying over the Southern Alps. I was in for a month of dramatic scenery and this was a suitable taster. The plane flew almost directly over Mounts Cook and Tasman and there followed vast glacial u-shaped valleys which led down to the equally vast Canterbury plains. The view immediately conjured memories of the *Lord of the Rings* films which I think were filmed in a number of locations on New Zealand's spectacular South Island.

I was starting my trip to New Zealand in Christchurch about two-thirds the way up the east coast of the South Island. New Zealand was originally divided into provinces and Canterbury was the province of which Christchurch was the capital. More recently the provinces have been replaced by regions.

I had always wanted to visit New Zealand. My first knowledge of the country came from the British Lions Rugby Tour of 1971. Being brought up in Melrose in the Scottish Borders, rugby was the sport I followed and as a twelve-year-old I was a passionate supporter. In those days tours lasted three months, from mid-May until mid-August, despite all the players being amateurs and therefore having to take time off work. They would involve matches against all the New Zealand provinces and that is where I became familiar with many of the romantic sounding place names: Wanganui and King

Country, Waikato, Otago, Marlborough and Nelson, Hawkes Bay, Taranaki, Bay of Plenty etc.

The match against Canterbury, played at Christchurch on 19th June 1971, became notorious as one of 'dirtiest' games of rugby ever played. Rugby was very much the national sport of New Zealand and with the Lions winning their first eight matches of the tour with some ease it became clear to the New Zealanders that a major challenge lay ahead in the Test Matches against the famous All Blacks. The match against Canterbury, the holders of the Ranfurly Shield, New Zealand's main domestic competition, was seen as the Lions' first big challenge. While the Lions managed a narrow victory, the main talking point was the alarming level of thuggery which took place during the match. I still remember the picture in the newspapers (that was how I mainly followed the tour, there being no live television coverage while the radio commentary in those days was distinctly crackly) of the battered face of Sandy Carmichael, the Scottish prop forward, coming off the field. The match cost the Lions the loss of two props to injury – Carmichael and the Irishman Ray Mcloughlin took no further part in the tour. Still the Lions went on to record a famous victory in the Test series winning two, losing one and securing an all-important draw in the final test in Auckland. As a Scot, I remember being proud that the crucial try scored in the victory in the First Test was by another Scottish prop forward, Ian 'Mighty Mouse' Mclauchlan. Apologies for that diversion into rugby history but it was an important part of my childhood while rugby is a central part of New Zealand life. Every town and village I passed through on my travels had a rugby ground.

The final section of the flight once you have cleared the Southern Alps is over the empty plains of Canterbury – I say empty but this is vast agricultural land. Outside of Christchurch, Canterbury is primarily devoted to farming – powerful Canterbury farmers in rugby's amateur days would make up the majority of the province's rugby team. The topography is largely featureless from the air until you approach Christchurch which sits just in from the coast. Its port is Lyttleton which sits in a sheltered bay behind the Port Hills, where there are some smart residential areas. It's worth taking a trip up on the Christchurch Gondola which gives you a fine view from the top over the city and the Canterbury plains on one side and Lyttleton Harbour on the other side. To the south of Christchurch, the Banks Peninsula is also worth a visit. It is a lovely drive down to the picturesque town of Akaroa which also has a pretty 9 hole golf course.

**The view over to Lyttleton Harbour from the
top of the Christchurch Gondola**

The first thing you notice about Christchurch as you take the short journey from the airport into the city is the amount of road and building works. This is the result of the devasting earthquake of 2011. The city is a tragic mix of areas of incredible beauty and areas of ugly building works. My visit was thirteen years after the quake and the effects are likely to be still visible in another thirteen years. Perhaps the most obvious reminder is the cathedral, a magnificent Victorian construction designed by Sir George Gilbert Scott, but now an imposing building surrounded by scaffolding. The foundations were laid in 1864 and the cathedral was consecrated in 1881. It had survived a number of earthquakes in its history but none as devasting as that of 2011. While work on stabilising the structure has been successfully completed, at the time of writing funding problems have left question marks about the completion of the whole project so, for the moment, the incomplete structure sits in the centre of the city as a poignant reminder of the tragedy.

I stayed in buildings which used to be the university near the city centre. The university had to be relocated and the buildings have been sympathetically restored and now comprise a hotel, restaurants and cafés. One feature of the city, the wonderful botanical gardens, has survived the earthquake. The gardens are very much part of the city and have a tranquil air about them. My other recommendation would be to take the tourist tram on which you can have dinner and tour the central streets while you eat.

There is a whisky distillery in central Christchurch – the Spirits Workshop. It is worth a visit though the location is unremarkable and it is in truth a distillery which makes whisky amongst a range of other spirits. The mash for its whisky comes from a brewery. It is a small business run by young enthusiasts but unlikely to be a significant player in the market. The main whisky attraction in

Christchurch is a business of a different sort. Michael Fraser Milne was born in the small Speyside town of Keith and moved to New Zealand over thirty years ago where he spotted the opportunity for Scotch Malt Whisky and together with his wife established the *Whisky Galore* brand. They opened their first shop in 2003 and now have large premises including extensive tasting facilities, all decked out in smart tartan. Their daughter, Siona, is now also increasingly involved in the business. They make regular visits to Scotland to keep up to date with developments, hold frequent special events at their premises and are very active on social media. I had an enjoyable morning and lunch chatting to Michael and Siona.

While their business mission is to introduce Scotch (and other whiskies) to New Zealanders, my motive in meeting Michael was to understand a little about how the industry was developing in New Zealand. Michael knows everyone there is to know so in this respect Christchurch was the perfect place to start my tour. He was able to point me in the right direction and provide some introductions. What was clear to me quite quickly was how small and niche the New Zealand industry currently is. That is in no way to denigrate the distilleries that are developing, simply to note that it is early days, much earlier even than Tasmania.

I had also decided not to play golf in Christchurch – there are a couple of clubs that could be ranked in New Zealand's Top 20 – Clearwater and Christchurch Golf Club. Clearwater is a modern resort course but I was tempted by Christchurch Golf Club as it is the second oldest in New Zealand and I had heard that in the clubhouse you can see the clubs used by Bob Charles, probably still New Zealand's most famous golfer, when he became the first left-hander to win the Open at Royal Lytham and St Annes in 1963. But I had to make sacrifices and choices – there would not be time in my insufficient four and a half weeks to play every golf course. It was time to head south.

The magnificent Victorian Opera House at Oamaru

The 9th green at Chisholm Links high above Tomahawk Beach

CHAPTER 10

SOUTH OTAGO

MY DESTINATION WAS Dunedin where I wanted to play the world's most southerly links golf course. Being a Scot, born in Edinburgh, I always had Dunedin as a must-visit place on my New Zealand tour and I wasn't disappointed.

First, however, there is the small matter of the four-and-a-half-hour drive down the east coast to get there. The first couple of hours to the regional town of Timaru are not actually close to the coast and the drive cannot be described as scenic. The road is dead straight with a few crossings of the railway line, which follows the same course, providing the only occasions when you need to use your steering wheel. The countryside could be described as 'flatter than flat' with the Southern Alps looming some hundred kilometres inland. Timaru is a large service town for the surrounding agricultural industries but from a tourist perspective the town of Oamaru, an hour further down the coast, is much more interesting. It is a small town of about 14,000 but it spreads itself along the coast and onto the hill behind. Here the attraction is surprisingly not the seafront, which hasn't been that well developed and is largely industrial, but the town itself. The main street is a wide avenue – 'boulevard' would not exaggerate its grandeur. It contains some extraordinary Victorian architecture, the most striking of which is probably the Opera House. Yes, Oamaru has its own Opera House and it is a magnificent building. But it is one of many built by wealthy grain and wool merchants from about the 1860s to the 1880s from the local white limestone, which makes them all the more magnificent-looking. There are numerous commercial buildings of similar style in the harbour precinct which is now home to many shops and cafés and is the main tourist centre. Nearby is the Blue Penguin Colony which attracts many visitors and you should leave time to walk around the beautifully tended public gardens – they are small by the standards of some of New Zealand's famous Botanical Gardens but beautifully tended with many points of interest including a bronze statue by the Scottish sculptor Thomas Clapperton and a Chinese Garden built as a tribute to the early local Chinese community.

Another surprise for me was to learn that Oamaru is the world's unofficial headquarters of 'steampunk'. Now, I suspect that many of my readers are not familiar with Steampunk. I have to admit that I wasn't either but was sufficiently intrigued to visit the town's Steampunk Museum. Steampunk describes itself, somewhat tautologically, as 'retro-futuristic', an art genre which blends the aesthetics of 19th century steam technology with elements of science fiction and fantasy. I'm not sure if that description helps so I suggest you head for your preferred search engine and see what turns up. I will not attempt to describe some of the features in the museum – my most vivid memory was going through a door into a room to find an elderly Australian gentlemen standing looking a bit bewildered. He looked up when he saw me come in, shook his head and said 'there's some weird things in here, mate'. He was not wrong.

I can justify my inclusion of Oamura in this chapter as there is a whisky connection which I will describe later. It is also home to the North Otago Golf Club which sits high above the town and which looked attractive if otherwise unremarkable. There is much else to see nearby particularly inland towards Duntroon Village in the

Waitaki Valley. The area is geologically important and there are many famous fossil sites as well as the elephant rocks, massive hummocky formations of limestone which, as their name suggests, look like elephants. I then decided to head for the Moeraki Boulders on the coast, having read about the scenic Danseys Road. I didn't, however, do my research properly. The road is about fifty kilometres so I thought I had plenty of time. It starts quite narrow as you head up into the mountains and after a bit it becomes a dirt track so you need to slow down. Surely the surface would improve? I thought about turning back but decided not to. The surface didn't improve and the mobile phone signal soon disappeared. I have to say that having no bitumen is one thing but the combination of no bitumen and no phone signal is quite another and not good for those of a nervous disposition. I'm not normally that adventurous. I persevered. The road climbed to over 3,000 feet and there were some steep gradients. The scenery was magnificent though I have to admit that I was not fully in the mood for appreciating it. I wouldn't have liked to have broken down and I only met one other car on the slow fifty-kilometres journey. It was with some relief that I reached a (relatively) main road and headed for the picturesque coastline just north of Dunedin. The Moeraki Boulders on the beach are not as imposing as the elephant rocks but it is a pretty area – the first stretch of New Zealand coastline I had properly explored.

Dunedin sits in an attractive position at the head of the sheltered Otago Harbour but also has a coastline directly facing due south onto the Southern Ocean. The city was established by Scottish settlers in the late 1840s, its name reflecting the Scottish Gaelic name for Edinburgh, Scotland's capital city. Gold and wool were what drove the city's early prosperity and it can boast the oldest university in New Zealand, the University of Otago. It is also home to some wonderful Victorian buildings, perhaps the most noteworthy being the main railway station completed in 1904.

I had expected lots of street names and place names to reflect the links with Scotland but perhaps not the extent of it. The main street is Princes Street and there is a George Street and a St Andrew Street so, as someone born in Edinburgh, I immediately felt at home. Even the suburbs were familiar with a Portobello and Musselburgh though, to be picky, you had to drive through Musselburgh out to Portobello whereas in Edinburgh it would be the other way around! The city is businesslike today rather than prosperous-looking though there is much new development along the harbour front. There for example a new, modern sports stadium has been built to replace the historic Carisbrook ground where the Lions played the first Test match in 1971.

The pretty Otago coastline north of Dunedin

Dunedin's other main attraction is the Otago Peninsula on the edge of the town, a thin strip of land which separates the enormous harbour from the Southern Ocean. It is a lovely area with two roads along it to Portobello, one tight against the harbour shoreline, the other high up with views both ways to the north and the south. On the morning I drove up it, the harbourside was beautifully still, the water like a mill pond while less than a mile away on the south-facing beaches the wind was up and the waves crashing onto the shore. There is much to enjoy in this small tract of land from the Royal Albatross Centre at the tip of the peninsula to the wild beaches on the south side and the architecturally extravagant Larnach Castle and its pleasant gardens sitting high up in the centre. There is actually also a small nine-hole links course on the peninsula called Otakou on the inner shore – it has sandy links turf but is tree-lined and set back from the coast.

There are three golf courses of note in Dunedin and I had to make choices as I only really had time to play one. The oldest is Otago Golf Club, dating from 1871, and can lay claim to being the oldest not only in New Zealand but in the southern hemisphere. Otago Ladies Golf Club, established in 1892, is also the oldest Ladies club in the southern hemisphere and the two clubs moved to the existing Balmacewen site in 1896. The course sits on a hill in the north of the city near the university and the botanical gardens. It's a smart parkland layout with some steep elevation changes. The clubhouse is attractive and you can sense the history with trophies such as the Bruntsfield Medal and the St Andrew's Cross.

St Clair is a mix of tree-lined parkland and clifftop in the south of the city with the middle holes affording some wonderful views across the Southern Ocean. But I headed for Chisholm Links, just up the coast from St Clair overlooking the large St Kilda beach.

Chisholm Links is and has been for most of its existence the world's most southerly links golf course. However, this was not always the case because between the early 1970s and 2018, that claim to fame belonged to Southland Golf Club at Oreti Sands, near Invercargill some two hundred kilometres to the south west. The story of Oreti Sands is a parable for the challenges that face golf courses in remote areas. New Zealand is a remote country and Invercargill is its most remote city with a population of just over 50,000, considerably less than half that of Dunedin. The course sat on a remote piece of links, a mix of dunes and pine forest, a totally natural site full of native grasses. It had always struggled but received a grant in 2008 to upgrade it. However, membership levels and green fee income was never sufficient to maintain it and sadly it closed in 2018. I didn't visit – I probably would have if it had still been there – but I gather that you can still walk around the site and see what remains of the layout.

Chisholm Links has the advantage of being ten minutes from the centre of Dunedin. The entrance is rather unprepossessing as it is next to a sewage works. I had rung to say that I would ideally like to play on a Sunday afternoon and was told that would be no problem. The course was developed in the 1930s and today is the home of Chisholm Park Golf Club and has a modern, rather uninspiring clubhouse. On the Sunday I visited in February, the height of summer, the course was quiet with only a couple of other groups out on the course.

It is a very classic old links and while the condition was not first class, the terrain and turf allows it to survive without, I suspect, a large greenkeeping team which would be unaffordable. The reception was friendly. I was able to hire clubs and I played on my own. The course can be divided into three sixes; the first a little inland, the second rising towards and along the coast and the final six on lower land to the south west. The middle section is definitely the highlight both in terms of the views and the golfing challenge.

The first 6 holes are certainly not without character. The first is a slightly strange dog-leg around a tree which reminded me a bit of the 1st at Goswick. The third is a driveable Par 4 (even for me) downhill but to a raised green so very difficult – maybe the second at Cruden Bay is a comparison. The holes are slightly overlooked by housing the other side of an unattractive brown fence so it is not an environment to lift the soul. This begins to change however, as you head up the hill to the short Par 3 7th and the long, extreme dog-leg Par 5 8th where, when you reach the green, you feel as if you are on top of the world as you look down steeply to the slightly scarily-named Tomahawk Beach below. And scary is a good adjective to describe the next par 4. It's only about 350 yards and dead straight but you certainly can't go left! Those with vertigo are advised to keep to the right of the pin – its position on the day I played was only a few yards from the cliff. It's perhaps not surprising that it is Stroke Index 2 – I took a nervous six strokes to complete it. There follows a fun downhill Par 3, suitably called 'The Crater' and then a snaking Par 5 which takes you back down the hill before an excellent Par 4 (Stroke 1) takes you back to the clubhouse. The final six holes are different again in character – they are set against the coast but you can't see the sea as there is a spur of land between the course and the beach so it is sheltered and mainly flat though the holes do have interest. 16 is yet another tricky short Par 4, 17 requires accuracy for both the drive and the second into the green which disappointingly sits next to the sewage works. 18 is a bizarre hole – it's a Par 4 of about 270 yards to a large green. Going for it feels dangerous but there isn't really an easy lay-up. Not the perfect 18th hole I feel. I wonder whether the course could start at 13 which means it would end with the best six holes and have the excellent tough par 4 12th as its 18th.

This isn't a great course but the six middle holes in particular will stick in the memory and it's a proper links test. You need to think about how your ball will bounce and play accordingly. I was lucky with the weather. It was a gloriously sunny day with a strong breeze which is what you want on a links course. I reckoned that I would have amassed about 32 Stableford points – I'm generally happy on a first visit with that sort of score.

Just as Bothwell could be regarded as where both golf and whisky in Tasmania was founded, the same can be said of Dunedin for New Zealand. I have referred to the Otago Golf Club being the oldest in the country while Dunedin has been central to both historical whisky distilling and its 20th-century revival. The arrival of Scottish settlers from the 1830s inevitably led to the development of a distilling industry but this was closed down in the 1870s by government regulation. Then in 1974, the Baker family opened Willowbank Distillery in Dunedin. It was sold first to Seagrams and then Fosters but fell victim to corporate priorities and closed in 1997, some years before the malt whisky boom.

Then in 2009 Greg Ramsay, yes, the same Greg Ramsay who had been involved in reviving Ratho Farm, developing the Nant Distillery and creating Barnbougle Dunes, got together a group of investors to buy the remaining stock of mature whisky from the now closed distillery. This comprised some 80,000 litres in 443 barrels apparently stored in an old aircraft hangar. It was moved to large bonded warehouses overlooking the harbour at Oamaru and a sales and marketing operation was set up to export the products. This was before any of the distilleries we will visit in New Zealand had been set up. The range was developed with some of the stock, for example, being transferred into wine barrels. They marketed the whiskies under a variety of brand names including *Wilson's* and *Milford* from the original Willowbank business as well as *The Otago* and *South Island*. I was drawn to the Sir Bob Charles 60th Anniversary Single Malt, apparently chosen by the great man himself. They now run a 'Cellar Door' from this site in Oamaru where you can visit for a tasting. My only sampling was from a private barrel that the owners of the magnificent bed and breakfast, Pen-y-Bryn Lodge, where I stayed in Oamaru. It certainly slipped down well after what had been a very fine meal.

However, a business based on buying old stock has a limited life so it is perhaps no surprise to learn that in 2020 a new distillery has been established and, in the intervening years, at least half a dozen whisky distilleries have emerged in New Zealand. The distillery has been built conveniently in the Speights Brewery in Dunedin which gives them a ready source for their mash. Speights is the historic brewery in the city founded in the 1870s which grew to become the biggest brewers in New Zealand first as New Zealand Breweries and then Lion Breweries. Today it is owned by the multinational Japanese brewer, Kirin, but the Speights brand name remains very strong in New Zealand. The brewery is a striking landmark building near the city centre and now includes an Alehouse pub which was doing a roaring trade when I visited.

Dunedin was always going to be an important destination for anyone visiting New Zealand with an interest in whisky and golf. Chisholm Links certainly delivered my links golf fix and it is now fitting that the city can again boast a whisky distillery.

The 9th green at the beautiful Arrowtown Golf Club

Jack's Point sits beneath the towering Remarkables mountain range

CHAPTER 11

CENTRAL OTAGO

IF YOU ARE visiting New Zealand, unless you give yourself at least two months, you have to make choices about where to miss out. The closure of Oreti Sands made me decide not to go down to Invercargill. The one temptation was the Auld Farm distillery at Scotts Gap about an hour to the north-west of the small city where, just as Oreti Sands was closing, the Auld family, big grain farmers for three generations, decided to set up their own distillery to produce gin and whisky. But instead, I headed straight for the well-known Queenstown in Central Otago where there is plenty of golf on offer and while its main beverage fame is for wine there is now an increasing amount of distilling.

Queenstown is very much the tourist centre of the South Island and is distinguished for its location as much as anything else. The city itself is architecturally disappointing, particularly after the delights of Oamaru and Dunedin, but the surroundings are extraordinarily beautiful. Its position on the shores of the enormous Lake Wakatipu and in the shadow of the towering Remarkables mountain range, now attracts nearly two million overseas visitors every year. I like to compare the scenery in New Zealand to that in Scotland as visually it can be similar. The difference is one of scale and some numbers will illustrate this: Loch Ness is about 750 feet deep (enough to hide a monster) while Lake Wakatipu is 1,250 feet deep; Ben Nevis is some

4,400 feet high and the Remarkables, by no means New Zealand's highest mountains, are over 7,500 feet.

There are a broad range of tourist types from the high-end to backpackers and a wide choice of activities from hiking, sailing, water sports, skiing in winter, golfing, and various adventure sports to the less active options of visiting vineyards or just eating and gawping at the scenery. Queenstown is also the centre for visiting the more remote areas of the South Island, be it the fjords in the south or the glaciers up the central spine of the island. Although this is a book on whisky and golf in New Zealand but I make no apology for mentioning my day trip to Milford Sound. It's only about seventy miles as the New Zealand crow flies from Queenstown to Milford Sound but it takes about three and a half hours to drive there as you head due south down into the vast farmlands of Southland to Mossburn, turn right and drive due west to Lake Te Anau, the largest lake in the South Island, even bigger than Wakatipu, and then turn right again and drive due north up to Milford Sound. I struck lucky again and didn't see a cloud all day, the ferry ride around the spectacular sound with its steep sides and gushing waterfalls and then the forty-five minute flight back to Queenstown over the Livingstone Mountains in a small ten-seater plane making it an unforgettable day.

I like also learning about a country's economy and wildlife and our guide that day was well-informed. Here are a few things I found interesting. Sheep farming has been in steep decline since the early 1980s with sheep numbers declining from seventy million to about twenty-five million; that's twenty sheep per head of population to just five today. There was an attempt to replace sheep with deer but this comes with problems as they strip the bark from native trees and step on the insects which are fodder for the native, protected Kiwi. Possums, which are protected in Australia, are considered a pest in

New Zealand as they eat native plants. I'm not an agriculturalist, economist nor an environmentalist but my observation is that, as with most things, there are no easy answers and very few obvious rights and wrongs. Most issues require balance and nuance. I'm sure I could draw a parallel with developments in golf and whisky but I will resist the temptation.

But back to business; I was here to investigate the golfing options and I had to make choices. I allowed myself two rounds of golf and had to decide which to play. Most ranking sites would put the top four courses on the South Island in the Queenstown area: Jack's Point, the Hills, Arrowtown and Millbrook. Add to this the obvious other option of Queenstown Golf Club at Kelvin Heights sitting on a small peninsula jutting out into Lake Wakatipu next to Queenstown. I was helped by a friend from England who lived in the area during the northern hemisphere winter though unfortunately due to a knee operation he was unusually not there when I visited. He was a member at one of the new courses, Millbrook, and one of the old, Arrowtown. I was immediately attracted by Arrowtown given its history while Millbrook was off limits while I was there as it was hosting the New Zealand Open the following week and not open to visitors. Geoff had told me that while the golf at Kelvin Heights was not of the same standard as the Hills or Jack's Point, the views were similar.

The Hills was built by a New Zealand entrepreneur in 2007 and is now an exclusive resort. By all accounts the location is spectacular and for your very expensive green fee you get not only a great golf course but a walk in a sculpture park – the course is peppered with large sculptures by the owner's son. Jack's Point is part of a new housing development on the road south out of Queensland and as Kelvin Heights had no tee times available, I decided to play there.

I was a little ambivalent about paying the substantial, though not outrageous, green fee for a modern course which is not normally my preferred type, but I was not disappointed.

I played in late afternoon having enjoyed a relaxing boat trip on the lake during the morning. It was warm and sunny with only a slight wind. I say this because I think that this was an important factor in my enjoying the round so much. The course sits in the shadow of the Remarkables on an exposed hill overlooking Lake Wakatipu and I would not have liked to have played it in bad weather. The greeting was friendly and relaxed and I continued my policy of taking a buggy on modern resort courses. The course starts inland and climbs the hill reaching the top at the Par 5 5th before heading down and along the edge of the lake. The back 9 wends its way back to the clubhouse.

It is a well-designed course and was a delight to play in the very benevolent conditions which I was fortunate enough to experience. I did, however, at times think that it could be very unforgiving in even a moderate wind as there were some big carries though there are multiple tee positions to cater for different standards of golfer. After a moderate but pleasing dog-leg Par 4 1st, it could be argued that holes 2-4 are a bit of a slog as they take you up the hill. 5, however, is a great par 5 and you are rewarded with a wonderful view from the green. 6 is a short par 4 which plunges down towards the lake and 7 is the frequently photographed downhill Par 3 which will be very difficult in any sort of wind. The mid round holes are all interesting on undulating land, all in different directions – there are two excellent par 3s at 11 and 13 – before you set off back to the clubhouse on the long par 5 14th. The golf course only occupies a small part of the land available and it has been built very sympathetically within its environment with natural grasses and tussocks while the stone walls frame the course pleasingly.

Jack's Point is a village with a golf course rather than just a golf course, with many more houses still to be built around a small lake and there are over twenty-five kilometres of walking and cycling trails. The clubhouse is corporate in feel so this is not my normal style but I enjoyed my round immensely, helped by the fact that I somehow managed two birdies and played to my handicap. I was playing off the front tees (still 6,300 yards) and, as I have said, the weather was very kind.

My score at Arrowtown the following day was nothing like as good despite similar weather conditions and a course of less than 6,000 yards. But to prove that how I play is not the main criterion as to how I judge a course, I loved it and if I wanted to play a course again in the area it would be Arrowtown. Arrowtown is a quaint heritage village sitting alongside a river and enveloped by mountains. It dates from the 1860s gold rush and, unlike Queenstown, most of its buildings have been beautifully preserved. The golf club dates from 1911 but moved to its existing site in the 1930s when the original nine holes were laid out. The second nine holes, which now play as the front nine, were added when some land beside the Arrow river across the road was acquired in the 1970s.

I was given a warm welcome with the mention of my friend Geoff's name helping and I set off on another warm, sunny afternoon. The course is gloriously picturesque – most places in the area are – and the hard dry turf put a premium on accurate shot making on nearly all of the consistently distinctive holes. You can see why it is known as 'Narrowtown'. The first hole sets the tone; it is a pleasingly shaped, relatively gentle downhill Par 5 but hitting the green requires a very careful shot, even from a short distance. The second green is more forgiving being fairly flat but there is plenty of interest before you get there with a steep drop in the fairway. I won't describe every hole but there are three good Par 3s on the front 9, the semi-blind 5th being my favourite as there seemed to be lots of options where to land it. The scariest drive is the 9th, a hole which defines quirkiness, as you have to attempt to drive high over a rocky outcrop to the right or aim for an insanely narrow strip of fairway between the aforesaid rocky outcrop and a pond. If you are successful in either of those endeavours you still have to hit the green which is protected by what the website calls a 'donga' which a dictionary tells me is 'a dry gully formed by the eroding action of running water'. Whatever it is, it's awkward.

If you are looking for a let-up in quirkiness on the back 9, you will be disappointed. It occupies a small tract of land with ridges and gullies and greens perched on hillocks. Every hole is an event. I loved the narrow valley of the Par 5 11th (perhaps this was because it was called 'Johnny Walker') while 12,13 and 14 are all relatively short Par 4s but all three are fraught with danger. In general, on the back 9 the greens are smaller and the implications of missing them more perilous. This is particularly true at the 18th where the entrance to the green looks disconcertingly narrow – I can tell you from experience that pulling it slightly left does not deliver a good outcome. This hole, somewhat appropriately, is called 'Look Out'. I have talked before about how I like holes being given names on a scorecard. I never found out why the 11th was called 'Johnny Walker' and the other holes had a very eclectic set of names from 'Garibaldi' and 'Waterloo' to 'Lady Fayre' and 'Nobby Dick'.

Arrowtown has a characteristic in common with Royal Ashdown Forest, Piltdown and Berkhamsted in that it has no bunkers but it really doesn't need them. In some ways bunkers might make it easier as they would catch slightly miss-hit shots which instead tend to kick violently away from the target. Arrowtown is pure golf and requires you to embrace the likelihood of bad bounces. But it is a course that requires thinking and rewards well struck shots. At 13 and 14 I hit good drives and, in both instances, had only about a 9 iron into the green. At 13 I hit a sweet second shot straight at the target and got a safe Par 4; at 14, I hit an uncertain one which fell off the green and I took 6.

**The new Cardrona Distillery has been
tastefully designed using local stone**

It was on the 11th that I saw a single player coming up behind me and I suggested we join up. This proved to be an enormous piece of luck as this was Alan Bradnock who was President of Takaka Golf Club on the north coast of the South Island which I planned to visit the following week. Alan was actually heading south and meeting his wife the following day to go on a walking holiday but he was delighted that I had Takaka in my sights and arranged for me to play in their Saturday competition, yet another example of the small golfing world we all inhabit. We had a very enjoyable seven holes comparing golfing stories. I left Arrowtown really wanting to play it again – it was a bit like leaving a restaurant wanting more.

I have described the scenery of the Queenstown area as being like that of Scotland but just dialled up several notches. It feels like a place where there should be whisky distilleries and they are beginning to emerge. The most recent is Scapegrace which sees its location as an important part of its proposition. The business actually started in Auckland but the founders spent several years looking for a site on which to build it. The distillery hadn't opened when I was there but I visited the site and it's certainly dramatic, sitting on the 45th parallel (mid-way between the Equator and the South Pole) at the foot of Mount Pisa and overlooking Lake Dunstan, fed by the Clutha river and easily accessible for those visiting the Queenstown area. The green-field site has allowed the business to design in sustainability to its process and this will be an important part of the brand's ethos. Distilling started in the summer of 2024 and by the time you read this the visitor centre is likely to be open.

But the first distillery in the area began in 2013, only about fifteen miles away as the crow flies over Mount Pisa and the Crown Range mountains but about an hour by car, as you have to drive back either south via Cromwell and Arrowtown then up the precipitous Crown Range Road, or north up to Wanaka and return south to Cardrona. Either way it is a scenic drive. Cardrona today is a small settlement at around six hundred metres but the ski resort goes up to three times that altitude. The attractive Cardrona Hotel is said to be one of the oldest in New Zealand, dating from the 1860s gold rush, and is worth a visit, as is the now famous 'Bra fence', a slightly out-of-context attraction just along from the distillery. Apparently, it started with a couple of tourists having a prank around the turn of the century and despite some local opposition has now become an established tourist attraction where anyone can hang their bra and give money to the New Zealand Breast Cancer Foundation.

I like distilleries with stories and the start-up of a new distillery is often associated with the vision and persistence of one individual. Desirée Reid was born just outside Dunedin but moved with her parents to a farm on the Canterbury plains when she was a toddler. She later bought her own farm and became part of Fonterra, the huge New Zealand dairy cooperative. But she always hankered after doing something else and after visits to America and Scotland sold her farm and decided she wanted to start a whisky distillery. She moved to Wanaka in Central Otago, believing that the popular tourist area with its natural landscape was a natural home for a whisky distillery. You can read her inspiring story of how a young dairy farmer opened New Zealand's biggest whisky distillery in her book *The Spirit of Cardrona*.

The distillery is situated just off the main road in a magnificent spot looking down the valley. The inspiration for the architecture of the buildings is a combination of Kentucky and Scotland using local stone and the effect is powerful and a little unexpected – perhaps only at Callington Mill had I seen so much effort put into the architecture and there it was mainly the restoration of historically important buildings. Certainly, as you approach, you sense an air of quality. The visitor centre is smart and there is a good restaurant and shop with tours of the distillery readily bookable.

Desirée had made many contacts in the distilling industry during her travels and made the best use of them. The mash tun and stills came from Forsyths in Scotland and Desirée credits Dave Pickerell, ex-head distiller at Maker's Mark, as a mentor, so again we see the mingling of expertise from America and Scotland. Initially all the distilling team were female, something quite unusual at that time in the world of whisky.

The business was sold to International Beverage Holdings, part of Thai Beverages in 2023 though, significantly, Desirée remains as Managing Director. From my visit, it was clear that the main product strategy is to increase production and lay down stock – I don't know the motivation for the sale but the cash challenge of looking to build significant stocks of 10 year+ aged whiskies is significant for a start-up family business. The purchase price was not disclosed but Desirée gets a rich multinational business with an established international sales network and IBH gets a ready-built quality whisky distillery with an enthusiastic workforce so it seems to make sense to me. While there are other Australasian distilleries making 10 year+ whiskies, many were happy with shorter maturation times. While the landscape and the weather may resemble Scotland in some ways, the big difference is the temperature range –15° centigrade in winter and up to 40° in summer is somewhat more extreme than you would get in Scotland. This clearly affects maturation and leads to a much bigger angels' share. Some distilleries call this maturing 'more quickly'. Certainly, it will mature differently. The business is certainly well-positioned to get access to quality casks with its Kentucky connections and the local vineyards providing a ready supply of ex-Pinot Noir barriques.

The New Zealand Tourist Site already advertises the Queenstown area as the home of 'the ultimate adventure bucket list'. I have already noted that it has the top four rated golf courses on the South Island; soon, with the opening of Scapegrace, it will have two of the biggest whisky distilleries as well so will also become a 'must' destination for the whisky and golfing tourist.

It is easy to work out the prevailing wind at Hokitika

The new distillery at Reefton has plenty space

CHAPTER 12

WANAKA, HOKITIKA AND REEFTON

THIS CHAPTER WILL cover quite a wide area from Wanaka, which could actually be part of the last chapter on Central Otago, up through the glaciers to the West Coast region and the pretty Buller District to the north. It's about five hundred kilometres from Wanaka to Reefton – about seven-to-eight hours of driving but there is plenty to see on the way.

Wanaka is a smaller, quieter, smarter version of Queenstown. The town's setting on the shore of Lake Wanaka (itself a smaller version of Lake Wakatipu) is idyllic – the partially submerged 'Wanaka Tree' has become an internationally renowned feature of social media postings. There is plenty to do – don't miss the Transport Museum on the edge of the town which has a mind-boggling collection of trains, planes and automobiles and much, much more – but Wanaka is best enjoyed either with a brisk walk up Mount Iron from where you get magnificent views over the whole area or a more gentle stroll in either direction along the lake's delightful shoreline.

It has a golf club which is in the middle of the town – you can walk there from the shoreline – and I played the front nine from which you get lovely views over the town and the lake. The tree-lined, more 'parklandy' back nine looked pleasant but less interesting. The turf was good and the holes quite tight so, with the dry bouncy conditions, was quite challenging. This is not a destination golf course but like many small New Zealand clubs definitely somewhere to enjoy.

About thirteen kilometres along the south-west shore, you come to Glendhu Bay which is the site of a proposed new golf course development. Construction had just begun on my visit and the course is due to open in late 2025. The project includes a number of private residences. It's perhaps time to discuss an increasing characteristic of New Zealand golf – premium new developments. Arguably this is a worldwide trend, but given the relative size of New Zealand they are beginning to dominate the country's rankings. The Top 100 website for New Zealand has 12 of the top 15 ranked courses as ones which didn't exist thirty years ago. Only Paraparaumu Beach, Titirangi in Auckland and Arrowtown feature as 'old' clubs. Glendhu Bay is being developed by John Darby whose name is associated with many of these modern New Zealand courses, starting with Millbrook near Arrowtown and Clearwater in Christchurch in the 1990s to both the Hills and Jack's Point in Queenstown as well as a number near Auckland which we will discuss later in the book. His business, Darby Partners, now has its offices at Jack's Point. Other notable names involved are the late American hedge-fund billionaire, Julian Robertson, who built Cape Kidnappers in Hawkes Bay and Kauri Cliffs in the Bay of Islands, Gary Lane, who made his money in food manufacturing and bought Wairekei in Taupo and John Sax, a property developer who bought the Kinloch Club, also in Taupo. As well as Glendhu, there are many others in the pipeline involving a range of different personalities: well-known Queenstown entrepreneur, Sir John Davies, is planning a new golf resort at Hogan's Gully near Arrowtown; the former Prime Minister John Key and New Zealand cricketing legend Brendan McCullum (when he is not coaching the England cricket team) are behind a development in the Gibbston Valley near Queenstown; a golf-loving software magnate is building the Douglas Links north of Wellington while a Chinese billionaire is opening a resort with a golf course designed by Kyle Phillips, of Kingsbarns fame, at Muriwai Downs north of Auckland. I could go on and will discuss Tara Iti and Te Arai in Chapter 16. There are many different business models but generally a few common characteristics: all require very significant investment capital and none can survive on green fee income alone while in all cases green fees are very expensive. There is obviously a range of prices depending on time of year and time of day but the range is probably between £150 and £400 per round (say US $200-500). In both Australia and New Zealand there are different rates for international visitors than New Zealand residents, something which in my view makes sense and which I see beginning to happen in the U.K. I won't comment further on this at the moment only to say that at the course which I am going to feature in this chapter, I paid the full green fee of $30 NZ – less than £15 sterling and it was wonderful.

The drive up the east coast from Wanaka takes you through glacier country, the two most famous being Fox Glacier and Franz Joseph. It's a great place to visit and there are numerous walks and flights available across the glaciers and over Mounts Cook and Tasman. I did two walks: the famous circular walk around Lake Matheson where if the weather is right and you are lucky (I was) you can see the reflection of the mountains in the stillness of the lake (it is often featured on New Zealand Tourist Board literature) and the climb up to Lake Wombat. I couldn't resist its name. In truth Lake Wombat itself is nothing more than a very peaceful large pond but the walk through the rainforest is atmospheric and I was excited to come across some of the rare blue toadstools which I was later shown are featured on the NZ $50 dollar note.

Much of the drive up the west coast does not feature the coast and the first main coastal town you reach is Hokitika, just under a hundred miles north of Franz Joseph. I was headed here as it has one of the relatively few true links golf courses in New Zealand; in fact, this area has three of the eight 'true links' in New Zealand, the other two being a little further up the coast at Westport and Karamea. The Mahinapua Links at Hokitika Golf Club is best of the three; Westport has a tree-lined feel and the nine hole at Karamea is charming but not in the same league as a golfing test.

The semi-submerged Wanaka Tree

Hokitika is an attractive, bustling seaside town with some impressive buildings. It was a busy Gold Rush port and also later famous for being the home of New Zealand's first licensed air service in 1934. There is still a small airport today. I stayed in a bed and breakfast called The Fire Station – it had been the old fire station and had been wonderfully converted into high quality accommodation. I even had an old fire engine on the street outside my window. The huge beach is very rugged – the west coast of New Zealand is not the best place for a gentle swim as the waves can be powerful and the currents are strong. Walking along the beach you are accompanied by the constant roar of the sea and you are very aware of the power of nature. You are also aware of some extraordinary beach art. Because of the powerful waves and currents there is an enormous amount of driftwood washed up all along the coast and at Hokitika this has become a focus for artists to create extraordinary driftwood sculptures of all manner of things. The annual Driftwood and Sand Festival has become an important date in the town's calendar.

The golf course, sometimes known as Mahinapua Links after the shallow lake at the mouth of the Hokitika river, is located appropriately along Links Road to the south of the town. The club dates back to 1906, significantly the same date as the railway reached the area, and is set along a narrow strip of links next to the beach but protected from the fairly constant winds coming off the Tasman Sea by a line of trees, most of which are leaning dramatically in an easterly direction. Looking inland you have the imposing background of the Southern Alps which adds to the drama of the location. The clubhouse is functional-looking rather than attractive. It was clear that finding a time to play would not be a problem but I wanted to hire some clubs and after a few text conversations with club officials I met Simon who unlocked a cupboard which contained a hotchpotch of clubs and bags. He told me to help myself to whatever I fancied – mix and match was very much the order of the day – and put the green fee in the honesty box. We had an enjoyable chat about Scotland and he wished me an enjoyable round while he returned to his work in the town. A two ball was just going off and I followed them out.

The clubs were not the latest models of Taylormade or Callaway which I had hired at the likes of Jack's Point. They probably dated from the early post-persimmon period and took a bit of time getting used to but after a few holes I had got into my stride. In fact, I think we can worry too much about whether we have the right clubs. I became rather fond of my 23 degree 'Nickent 3DX Ironwood' which I began wielding to some effect. It's not a long course – some 6,000 yards – has a Par of 71 and I played round in 80 which for a 11/12 handicapper is pretty good. Would I have scored better with a brand new set of Taylormades? I doubt it.

This is an authentic links experience with undulating fairways and firm greens. Despite the 'shelter' of the trees, wind was a constant factor and the noise of the sea a constant companion. It's a narrow stretch of land so there is not much separating the holes, and the rough was fairly gentle which probably helped my score. The course, slightly unusually, makes its way out to the end and back to the clubhouse at 14 before you play a four-hole loop to finish.

There are not any really standout holes – this is understated proper links golf. I did, however, enjoy the Par 3 10th where you stand with your back to the beach and hit directly inland; despite the narrow strip of land the direction of the holes is often subtly different. The 14th back at the clubhouse has an awkward bunker immediately in front of the green and is called Thompson's Corner in memory of a Scottish club member. Looking at pictures in the clubhouse, there seem to have been lots of Thompson members.

All this for £15 – the likes of Kauri Cliffs and Cape Kidnappers charge over £400 for a very similar 'product'. Is Kauri Cliffs really more than twenty-five times better than Hokitika? It depends what you enjoy and I enjoy links golf and Hokitika is classic links course. I will share with you my Kauri Cliffs experience later in the book but if I had to play one of these courses regularly, I would choose Hokitika as it is likely to provide a more varied golfing challenge.

Hokitika makes a pleasant holiday destination as there is plenty to do – I drove inland to walk around the scenic Hokitika Gorge with its steep white granite cliffs and brilliant turquoise waters. The scenic Lake Kaniere is a popular holiday spot and there are many other lakes and rivers and walks in the foothills of the mountains. I had noticed in the town numerous shops selling jade – the Māori word is *pounamu* – and it is these glacial waters which are the main source of this precious stone. Hokitika's problem is that it is very far from anywhere – over three hours from Christchurch, four from Nelson and over five from Wanaka. The golf club really is a hidden gem.

I headed north up the coast, my next destination being Nelson, but on the way I wanted to take a detour inland to Reefton to visit a new whisky distillery. In this next section you are much closer to the coast and there are some attractive vistas especially north of Greymouth and it is worth stopping for a break to visit the limestone 'pancake rocks' and blowholes at Punakaiki.

Reefton is one of very few inland towns in this part of New Zealand and is small with a population of under 1,000 but it has a rich history. It is attractively located in a valley by the Inangahua River in the Victoria Conservation Park. Like so many places, it dates back to the 1860s/1870s gold rush. The wealth created by gold mining led to Reefton's other main claim to fame as the first town in the southern hemisphere to have a public supply of electricity after entrepreneurial mining engineers saw the potential to create hydroelectric power from the fast-flowing river. It was also an important rail junction in the West Coast region. The town today has a prosperous feel to it and rather like Arrowtown has many heritage buildings which have been carefully restored and maintained. Most are not museum pieces but remain working establishments: shops, tearooms, hotels. While it is small, it seems likely to grow over the next few years as gold mining is returning and a recent discovery of antimony, a strategic mineral used in semi-conductors and military devices, is likely to increase employment.

So, it can't be said that the opening of a distillery in 2017 is critical to the future of a small town but it is already a well-known business within the community. The founder and Chief Executive Patsy Bess was born in Reefton but moved to Christchurch as a child in the late 60s though returning to Reefton for frequent holidays. Returning to the town of her birth with her husband, Shane Thrower, she saw the opening of a distillery as a means of revitalising the town and held a series of community forums and managed to raise the seed capital via a share-equity offer to launch the business. It started on a small scale in the town and in 2020 they raised further capital to purchase a site on the edge of the town which would enable a significant increase in production. The original site in town remains as a tasting room and retail outlet.

The early focus was gin with the Little Biddy brand named after a famous Reefton resident, Bridget Goodwin, an Irish migrant who became a gold prospector, with fruit liqueurs and vodka following in 2018. The gin has by all accounts been a success and has been the early engine of the business's growth. The new site was formally opened in September 2022. I visited about eighteen months later and was shown around by Sean, a Scot from Aberdeenshire, who had worked with Michael Fraser Milne in Christchurch and was getting some hands-on experience working at the new distillery. The operation was still very manual though the equipment was modern and there was plenty space. There are plans for maturation warehousing on the site. There seems to be plenty of whisky knowledge in the business with the Distillery Manager having worked at the likes of Macallan and Tamnavulin while they have a whisky panel which comprises two current Scottish Distillery Managers as well as Michael Fraser Milne and Bill Lark so the business has good connections. Again, we see how the whisky industry likes to support start-ups.

The whisky brand is Moonlight Creek named after an area some thirty miles away which is the source of the water and which in turn was named after another gold prospector, a Scot named George Moonlight. It seems a strange name for a Scot. Apparently his full name was George Fairweather Moonlight and he was born in Glenbervie in Aberdeenshire. The first casks were filled in September 2022 and the combined efforts of the whisky panel and the production team helped the business win awards in the 'New Make' and 'Young Spirit' Rest of World categories at the World Whisky Awards in 2025.

They are looking to make available a three-year matured single malt from ex-bourbon casks and as well as experimenting with types of barley and manuka wood smoke to have a special edition with a distinctive New Zealand twist. I obviously haven't tasted any but the prospects look good.

Reefton is a quaint small town with a relaxed feel but with a noticeable vibrancy to it. The cafés and shops were bustling on the day I visited. Its relatively remote location means that it is the sort of town where the inhabitants have to make it what it is and the setting up of a whisky distillery is very much part of this. I sense that it will be embraced by the community. It was not surprising therefore to notice that the town has a '12 hole voluntarily run' golf course next to the river just north of the town. As I have said previously, if I have one regret about my itinerary it was that I didn't leave enough time to play courses like this.

A classic links look at Takaka

Evening light at Nelson Golf Club

CHAPTER 13

NELSON AND GOLDEN BAY

OUR FINAL VISIT on the South Island is to the Nelson area. As you make your way up to the north coast there are any number of scenic routes to take as you follow the meandering Buller river and pass through the Nelson Lakes National Park and the Mount Richmond Forest Park. Nelson is on the north coast but is actually the geographical centre of New Zealand. As you approach the city you see the vineyards which the area is well known for. The outskirts of the city are not particularly attractive but the city centre, around the cathedral just back from the coast, has a relaxed feel to it. This is a small city of under 60,000 inhabitants. Christ Church Cathedral is an imposing building set up on a hill but it has a chequered history and today still divides opinion with its modernist gothic revival style. A stone cathedral was built in Victorian times and consecrated in 1887 but was badly damaged by an earthquake in 1893. An ambitious new design was started in the 1920s but the strengthening of building regulations following another earthquake brought that to a halt and the existing building was begun in the 1950s and completed in 1967. The mixture of Victorian stone and the concrete bell tower is certainly distinctive though I gather there are concerns about the structure's ability to withstand any future earthquakes.

Nelson has a pleasant links course set by the sea near the airport. It is set on flat land and the removal of numerous trees in recent years gives it a conventional links look and feel. I had a short walk around it but didn't have time to play as I was headed for Takaka overlooking Golden Bay some hundred kilometres to the north. When I told the owners of the bed and breakfast this they said, 'Oh! You're going over the hill. Remember to count the corners; there's one for every day of the year.' I didn't really understand what they were getting at and the first part of my journey up the coast was fairly straightforward but then the road has to climb 'the hill' which, it transpires, is around 2,000 feet and it does this by way of a succession of dramatic switchback corners both up and down. I didn't count the corners but I can well believe that there were 365. Takaka is a town on the main road at the foot of the hill on the other side but I was headed to the golf club just a few miles away on the coast at Pohara which sits looking out over the attractive and peaceful Golden Bay. As if to please me, on the way I passed the Kiwi Spirits Distillery which I popped in to have a look at. It is actually the oldest of the existing New Zealand distilleries dating from 2002 but it remains a small craft operation producing a range of spirits including whisky. A bar with a shop is open daily for you to peruse and taste their various offerings. It was early morning when I visited and I was driving so I was only able to have a quick look around and buy a miniature of their Waitui Single Malt aged for eight years in manuka honey oak barrels. It is pleasant: rich and sweet. The only other feature is that it calls itself 'whiskey' rather than 'whisky' in line with all other New Zealand and Australian producers. The convention is that only in the United States and Ireland is whisky spelled 'whiskey'. Maybe it was a misprint.

Alan Bradnock, the Club President, whom I had met at Arrowtown, had told me that the 'haggle' would start at midday. 'Haggle' was not a word I associated with golf but my friend Geoff had mentioned it and I began to realise that it is very much part of the golfing lexicon in New Zealand. Embracing different terminology is an enjoyable part of learning the culture of a different country. I've already mentioned trolleys being trundlers but I also had to learn new terms for coffee. This allows me again to talk again about coffee which I increasingly think can be compared to whisky in its numerous variations and complexity. I soon realised that Australia and New Zealand have different coffee language to Europe. I like smallish black coffee – I tend to ask for a 'small Americano' in the U.K. I soon realised that this required me to ask for a 'Long Black' which in Americano terms is quite short; a 'Short Black' is an espresso. If you want a longer Long Black you just ask for some hot water on the side. Very sensible. I have to say that the coffee in Australia and New Zealand is generally excellent – on average much better than in the U.K. I remember on my first day in Hobart enjoying the coffee in my hotel and then on a trip to Bruny Island stopping at the small ferry terminal where there was a very unassuming looking café. I wanted a coffee but felt that it wouldn't likely be much good. Eventually I risked it and it was superb and the vast majority of the coffees I ordered on my trip were good, a much higher proportion than would be the case in the U.K. though the U.K. is improving.

I continue to read about coffee and how to make the perfect cup. As in whisky there are so many variables: the beans, the grind, the tamping pressure, the extraction time, the temperature of the water. The beans are affected by their 'terroir' but also how they are roasted. Some will create a blend of beans to create a balance of flavour – does that sound familiar to whisky makers? I learned that the major difference between an Americano and a Long Black is that for the former you add hot water to an espresso while for a Long Black you add espresso into hot water. Like whisky there are endless variables. The search for the perfect coffee is, like the search for the perfect whisky, a perpetual one. And I would argue that there isn't such a thing as a perfect whisky or a perfect cup of coffee. I return to my contention that it is all about the context of the moment of consumption and the particular needs at that time of the consumer. Just as I don't have a favourite whisky – I sometimes want a light smooth one while other times I want a hit of peat – I can't say that I have discovered the perfect coffee. What I want at breakfast is probably milder than the espresso I want after a heavy lunch. The variety is the essence of the appeal of both whisky and coffee... and indeed golf courses.

The unusual bell tower at Nelson Cathedral

Alan had said that I would be looked after by Warwick Dobbie at Takaka. I had arrived in good time and there was little activity but I noticed a smart set of clubs on a trolley (sorry, trundler) sitting outside the starting hut. The clubhouse was open but not much was happening. Gradually a few people started arriving and when I said I had been invited to join the haggle they seemed pleased and said that Warwick would be there in due course. Visitors joining the Saturday competition was not unusual. Warwick, it transpired, lived some distance away at the northern end of Golden Bay and he arrived just as arrangements were being made. The bag of clubs indeed were for me. They had been leant to me by the greenkeeper who, I was told, was a good golfer. They were certainly a good set of clubs.

Warwick and I were drawn in a fourball against Neil and Carl; as well as a Stableford competition we played a match within our match. It looked tricky to start with as Carl hit the ball a prodigious distance but by the second nine, Warwick and I had steadied up and Carl's radar began to become a little faulty so we eventually saw them off.

Takaka is a 9-hole course with two tees on a number of the holes; I remember 10, 11 and 13 in particular being quite different on the second 9. There is one Par 5 and three Par 3s. The land is natural links but the low-lying terrain of the course with the sea on one side and the marshy lands of the estuary on the other estuary has led to quite a lot variation in grasses. There has been an invasion of kikuyu grass in some places which makes for a very different game. The members were aware of the problem – the best quality holes were those by the sea with authentic links turf.

The club dates from before the first World War and originally the location was on farmland nearer the town – it moved locations a couple of times. The move to the seaside location began in the 1960s but required the removal of a great deal of gorse, a task which the members set about themselves. They even moved the old clubhouse before the existing structure was built in the 1970s.

It's a delightful spot overlooking Golden Bay. The first two holes take you away and then back to the clubhouse to the east, both Par 4s where the challenge is controlling your second shot to the green in the dry running conditions. The first hole is called 'swamp' the second 'hump' and the third is a delightful Par 3 next to the beach called 'hollow'. Humps and hollows are indeed a feature of this part of the course. The 3rd/12th sets up delightfully, is only about 150 yards but I missed the green on both loops. The 4th/13th hole is also memorable, a short Par 4 of some 300 yards but there is a very pronounced ridge running all the way from the tee to the green. There are many ways of playing the hole: take it on, play safe short and right or go left which suggests more danger but is probably the easier angle to the tricky green which sits in another hollow. These options make it a great hole. 5/14 and 6/15 are two dog-leg Par 4s, both requiring care up to and back from the estuary, and 7/16 a long Par 3 which was also, on the day I played, back into the wind. Having missed the green at 3/12 on both rounds I was delighted to hit the green on this near 200 yarder on my second loop. 8/17 is a long Par 5 back to the clubhouse before you have to end your round playing 'Whoopee', the rather engaging name for the Par 3 9th/18th, a short 120 yard Par 3 where there is nowhere good to miss. The green sits up on a mound and is bigger than it looks, but in windy conditions requires a well-struck shot to hold the green.

I think we shook hands on the 17th, Carl having fallen foul of the out-of-bounds on the right (something he felt was unnecessary) but in truth, whatever the merits of that particular out of bounds, this is not a course where hitting the ball a long way helps unless you are also accurate. It's about the accuracy of your second shots, which can be helped by driving into the best position, and good putting.

Afterwards I was invited into the clubhouse to tuck into some sandwiches and drinks. There was a short prize-giving – no one from our group featured – and plenty of banter. I was introduced and I presented the club with one of my books. This all felt to me like real golf in New Zealand and could have been any small club in Scotland. Informal competitive golf. I like the description on the club's website of the Saturday competition: '*Play golf in a competitive yet social environment. Play all types of competitions: strokeplay, matchplay, par, stableford, pairs etc.*' That's is the sort of golf I enjoy the best. Around the room there were the usual hard luck stories, the many 'if onlys', the teasing accusations of handicap bandits, the golf bores talking endlessly about their own game, the complaints from Carl about the out-of-bounds being in the wrong place; all these can be heard at clubs like Takaka all around the world. I felt very at home. And all was thanks to the coincidence of meeting the Club President on the back 9 at Arrowtown and asking him to join me. I headed back over 'the hill' taking on the 365 corners in good cheer.

More classic links at Paraparaumu Beach

The Wellington Cable Car

CHAPTER 14

PARAPARAUMU BEACH AND HAWKES BAY

I HAD BEEN in New Zealand for two and a half weeks when I crossed the Cook Strait from Picton to Wellington which was to be my first sight of the North Island. The ferry journey through the Queen Charlotte Sound and across the strait takes about three-and-a-half hours. I found Wellington confusing; it sits on the southern tip of the North Island but actually faces north across the bay. A little disorientating – as an inhabitant of the northern hemisphere I had only just, after six weeks, got used to the sun being due north at midday. I knew that I was planning to head up the west coast and assumed that meant me turning right as I faced the sea but in fact it was the opposite direction.

Wellington is known as the 'windy city' and it didn't let me down. During my six weeks in the southern hemisphere, the only significant rain I had seen was the storm in Melbourne which I had witnessed from my hotel at Tullamarine Airport. The forecast for my day in Wellington was not promising and, as predicted, a storm blew in bringing high winds and torrential rain. My plan had been to mooch around Wellington in the morning and then head for Paraparaumu Beach some forty-five minutes up the coast in the afternoon but on seeing the forecast I contacted the club and asked whether it would be possible to play the following day. They were very helpful and relaxed about it so I altered my plans accordingly, spending a wet morning at the impressive Te Papa Museum and in the afternoon, when the weather had relented somewhat, taking the old cable car up to the Botanical Gardens and walking back down the hill.

But my priority while in Wellington was always to play Paraparaumu Beach as I had heard that it was New Zealand's top links course. It is probably also New Zealand's top 'old' course. The other major club in Wellington is Royal Wellington which dates back to 1895 but actually only gained its Royal status as recently as 2004. Today's course, however, is even more recent than that, being completed in 2013. It sounds pleasant but it didn't excite me whereas Paraparaumu did. Warwick at Takaka had been a member and sang its praises and gave me an introduction to the General Manager. I drove the forty-five minutes up the coast and got there early in the morning as I had to drive on in the afternoon up to Napier on the east coast. I was very well looked after and as they were sanding the greens (they were still immaculate) they insisted on giving me a discount. The location itself is decidedly underwhelming. It is a classic piece of linksland but rather like Lytham St Anne's it is surrounded by houses and you can't see the sea which is about two blocks away. As at Royal Melbourne the quality of the course is not flattered by the views. That said, as you look over the course from the balcony of the elevated clubhouse the heart certainly stirs as you can see that this is a perfect piece of land for a golf course. There are no hills as such but equally, I don't think any hole could be described as flat – gentle, rolling dunes and subtle changes in elevation.

The club is not that old with the current course dating from the early 1950s. A course had been laid out on the land in the late 1930s but a general meeting of the Club held in 1949 agreed to build a new course to a design by Alex Russell of Royal Melbourne fame. Russell was descended from a family of farmers in Fife in Scotland and his parents moved from Melbourne to the United Kingdom in 1903 so he went to school at both Hindhead in Surrey and Glenalmond in Perthshire before finishing his education at the famous Geelong Grammar School near Melbourne. He returned, however, to study engineering at Jesus College, Cambridge just before the Great War broke out, his studies being interrupted as he went to serve with distinction on the Western Front. Returning to Australia, he won the first medal held at Royal Melbourne after the war.

He became a well-respected amateur golfer but it was Alister MacKenzie's famous 1926 trip to Royal Melbourne which made him famous as he became MacKenzie's design partner, tasked with overseeing the design of Royal Melbourne as well as other projects in Australia. It is not known how MacKenzie and Russell formed a friendship though they had similar experiences of both Cambridge University and war service. Just as MacKenzie had designed Royal Melbourne and left Russell to bring that design to fruition, so too did Russell submit the design for Paraparaumu Beach during a six-week visit in 1949 and then entrust the greenkeeper Jack Hunt to oversee its construction, only returning in 1952 to assess progress. Its final completion was in 1954.

It is said that his portfolio of courses did not include links but this is to misunderstand what is important to a golf course designer. Melbourne sand belt courses such as Royal Melbourne and his other creation, Yarra Yarra, are not links, but they are built on sandy soil which encourages the 'running game' which is behind the MacKenzie design philosophy. And that is what you get at Paraparaumu Beach.

The club has hosted some twelve NZ Opens. One of the most famous was the 2002 event, won by Craig Parry, as a certain Tiger Woods was in the field. Tiger had been persuaded by his caddy, Steve Williams, to fly over and support the event. Williams had learned his golf as a caddy at Paraparaumu Beach in the 1970s. Famous winners of the NZ open when it was held at Paraparaumu Beach include Peter Thomson, Bob Charles, Corey Pavin and Michael Campbell.

Napier's distinctive art deco architecture

I teed off by myself and hit an average drive up the right of a gentle dog-leg Par 4 and slightly mishit my 5 iron second which ended up just short of the front edge to the right, some forty-five feet from the pin. I had not had a chance to have a putt on the putting green and the greens were slightly sanded so I decided to have a few practice putts around the hole to give me a feel for the pace and my hired putter. I then walked back to my ball hoping for a good up and down to make my par. I didn't make par: I struck the putt and it never left the line of the hole, gently hitting the centre of the pin and dropping in. I was already loving Paraparaumu Beach.

The only disappointment was that this was obviously the highlight of my round and had come very early. There are, however, plenty more highlights on the course with one consistently good hole after another, all distinctive, all requiring thought and care. The quality of the turf and the greens was consistently good. The layout is two loops of nine; the first up the centre and returning via the inland side of the course and the second skirting the seaside and northern boundaries and then returning up the centre to the 18th green which sits directly below the clubhouse. This meant that you were continually assessing different wind directions. Many of the greens are raised and sometimes for a mid-handicapper like me, the smart play was to ignore the flag and just get it on the green. The course is not particularly long though with just three Par 5s and each of these under 500 yards this is a little misleading. There are some big Par 4s (3,4,11 and 17) and two of these will always be into the wind. The Par 3s are all excellent, perhaps the most distinctive being 16 which plays at an awkward angle across some wildly undulating land to a trickily shaped raised green. The long Par 4 17 is also memorable having a difficult drive and a split fairway; the easier right-hand side shortens the hole but the angle to the green requires you to fly it all the way and hope it stops.

I joined up after a few holes with a young Englishman who was working in a local sports centre. He was a good golfer, hitting the ball a long way, but he was also a bit wayward and the course caught him out on a number of occasions. Rather like Takaka, Paraparaumu Beach is not a course that can be overpowered by distance hitters.

I had played reasonably well though not made the most of my spectacular start and I would have loved to stay and play another eighteen but I had to head north.

My destination was Napier on Hawkes Bay, about halfway up the east coast of the North Island which required me to cross over the centre. It was an attractive drive though without any of the drama and majesty which I had got used to on the South Island. Why Napier? It's an attractive small city renowned for its art deco architecture, a result of it being rebuilt after a devastating earthquake in 1931, the art deco style being chosen for its simplicity and its strength. There is very little high rise building in the city.

In golfing terms Hawkes Bay is known for Cape Kidnappers, one of the two premium golf resorts in spectacular locations developed in New Zealand around the turn of the century by Robertson Lodges. It costs over £400 to play at Cape Kidnappers or its sister course Kauri Cliffs in the Bay of Islands. I had decided that I would play one of them to understand the proposition but not both. In the end I decided to play Kauri Cliffs, which I will describe in the penultimate chapter, for two reasons: the delay in playing Paraparaumu Beach would have meant that I would have arrived at Napier the night before and had to play Cape Kidnappers the following day without a chance to have much of a look around Napier, and secondly, I had heard from a number of people, including my friend Geoff, that the best views of Cape Kidnappers are those which you can view on the website, pictures obviously taken by drones and therefore not reflective of what you see as a golfer. At Kauri Cliffs, by contrast, you don't need drones to see the views. I can't verify this as I didn't visit Cape Kidnappers where I am sure that there are some dramatic views but I think there is probably some merit to this observation.

Napier is small and had an attractive long promenade along the seafront. I'm conscious that I have brought you here and have no golf or whisky to describe. Instead, I will conclude this chapter offering you a different angle on *Of Peats and Putts*. I visited Napier's attractive Botanical Gardens which are also small but situated on a dramatic slope at the back of the city. Originally laid out in Victorian times, they were not well looked after during the first part of the 20th century but since the late 1960s have been beautifully restored and manage to fit an interesting range of plantings into a relatively small space. It is time perhaps to discuss Botanical Gardens – I always make a bee line for them whenever I visit a city and I enjoyed numerous strolls around them on my trip. Indeed, let's put aside golf-course rankings for a moment. I will share with you my own rankings of the Top Botanical Gardens of Australasia.

I have visited gardens (some may not have been officially labelled 'botanical') in Melbourne, Sydney, Perth, Hobart, Christchurch, Dunedin, Queenstown, Oamaru, Wellington, Napier, Taupo and Auckland. They are all different, some of them integrated into the city like Melbourne, Sydney and Christchurch and others with more of a separate identity like Hobart and Napier. Some of the smaller ones are maintained by volunteers. At Taupo I was shown round its beautiful gardens by Marion who had a great pride for this delightfully peaceful space only a few minutes from her home. I won't give you a definitive ranking but here is my summary and my top three: I will discount Melbourne, Sydney and Perth as their scale is too large though they are still all magnificent; Auckland is also huge and its out-of-town location next to a motorway doesn't help; Christchurch does deliver city centre peace as does Wellington to a lesser extent and while Dunedin is pleasant, Queenstown Gardens are more about the lakeside location than the gardens themselves.

So Taupo and Oamaru take third equal place – both fairly small, the former less formal and more natural, the latter more varied with greater planting – Napier takes second place for transforming what looks like an unpropitious space into something very remarkable delivering enormous variety within a small space, but my No 1 ranked Botanical Garden in Australasia is Hobart which in my view has a bit of everything. It is big but doesn't feel so as there are so many different small spaces within it. It somehow combines scale with intimacy; managed planting with natural open spaces; a Japanese Garden, a French Explorer's Garden and even a Subantarctic Plant House.

The 5th green at Wairekei

The small stone bridges give Wairekei an 'Augusta' feel

CHAPTER 15

TAUPO

AFTER DIVERSIONS INTO coffe also e and gardens I can return to golf in this chapter but not whisky, the only North Island distilleries being in and around Auckland. However, I wanted to visit the central area of New Zealand famous for its geothermal activity and Lake Taupo, the largest lake in all of New Zealand, which also offers two famous golf courses; the Kinloch Club and Wairekei.

I had heard about places like Taupo and Rotorua and seen pictures of geothermal springs but nothing really prepares you for your first visit to the area. My drive from Napier over the Ahimanawa Range, extensive, rugged hills rather than mountains, had been somewhat slow as there were numerous roadworks. This was a result of Cyclone Gabrielle which had hit the North Island the previous February causing devastation from Auckland down to Napier, with the Hawkes Bay area hit particularly hard. There had been many landslides on roads all across the North Island. I have mentioned before how in New Zealand you are aware of the power of nature and this was yet another example. As you emerge into the Taupo area, a newcomer might observe what looks like smoke at regular intervals across the landscape. It is of course not smoke but steam emerging from the ground in what is the Taupo Volcanic Zone. It takes a bit of getting used to.

The Taupo Volcanic Zone sits on the Pacific Ring of Fire, a tectonic belt of volcanoes and earthquakes stretching from New

Zealand up through Indonesia, The Philippines and Japan and over to the west coast of the United States and down through Mexico, Peru and Chile. Earthquakes are central to the history of New Zealand as we have already experienced in Christchurch, Nelson and Napier. New Zealand sits on the boundary of the Pacific and India/Australia tectonic plates, hence its vulnerability to earthquakes. The big geological event which fashioned this area was a series of earthquakes in 1886 which led to the eruption of Mount Tarawera and the creation of Lake Rotomahana. It is extraordinary that this event happened less than 150 years ago. You can walk down Waimangu Valley with its gurgling geysers, emerald pools and atmospheric springs and take a boat trip on the lake and observe what is left of Mount Tarawera. The lake is peaceful until suddenly a geyser springs into life aggressively spouting out steam at 101.7° centigrade for a few seconds which it does regularly to a set cycle; this is called 'fumarolic' activity. It is startling to observe and for non-scientists like me quite bewildering.

There is much more to explore from Rotorua in the north of the area to the Huka Falls in Taupo itself. The town is spread along the north shore of the enormous lake and there are plenty of restaurants to choose from which overlook the waterfront. I mentioned the Botanical Reserve and this is perhaps the best place to view the lake as it is elevated. My sister had stayed with a family in the days of her student travels so I was lucky to be taken round these peaceful gardens by Marion whom I had met for coffee at her house nearby.

But I was here for golf and had to make the difficult choice between the Kinloch Club and Wairekei. The Kinloch Club is a Jack Nicklaus design and his only one in New Zealand. It sits a few miles south-west of Taupo in a quiet spot overlooking the lake and has a very rugged feel to it, perhaps not typical of Nicklaus courses. The terrain was sheep-grazing farmland and obviously volcanic but now has the look of a natural links or heathland but all the 'natural' features are entirely manmade. It looks fun and it looks tough – a bit like Jack's Point, you would want good weather.

A Māori building near Rotarua

You will have gathered by now that I chose to play Wairekei which may sound surprising as it is more of a parkland layout, though a very special one. For me, Wairekei was more convenient being on the edge of town and it is 30% cheaper for a visitor to play and I was intrigued by a golf course being combined with a nature sanctuary.

The story of Wairekei is interesting in a number of respects. It was built and opened in 1970 by the New Zealand government who wanted Taupo to have an internationally acclaimed golf course to attract tourism. At that time, New Zealand would not have been a renowned destination for golfers, perhaps Paraparaumu Beach and Titirangi in Auckland apart. The course design was assigned to Commander John Harris, a name that we have come across just once before in my books. Harris is less well known than the names of Colt, Mackenzie, Braid, Fowler and Simpson from the golden era as perhaps the age he worked in (he was born in 1912 and died in 1977) was not one of the most active in golf-course building. However, his family firm, Franks Harris Brothers was actually one of the first involved in golf-course construction (it had been established in the 1890s), undertaking projects for the likes of Colt and Fowler, so this was his introduction to golf-course design. The other reason he is less well known is that most of his work was abroad, being active in Denmark, France, Spain, the Netherlands and particularly Italy. It was at the delightful Menaggio and Cadenabbia on the banks of Lake Como that we encountered him in *Of Peats and Putts Continental*. Further afield he worked on projects in Barbados, Jamaica, Hong Kong, India, Singapore, Indonesia and Australia so he certainly got about. At Wairekei, he worked with Mike Wolveridge and five times Open Champion, Peter Thomson. Wolveridge was also an ex-professional golfer, the first Englishman to play on the US PGA tour, and together they formed a design firm in 1968 doing most of their work in Asia and Japan.

The course subsequently became private and after some changes in ownership, it was bought by Gary Lane, an Auckland businessman who made his money selling his food business to the American food giant Kraft. The course had not been well looked after and Lane set about restoring it to its former glory, getting Peter Thomson back to advise. Today, following a major upgrade to the greens about five years ago, Wairekei is regarded as one of the best conditioned courses in New Zealand. But the course's real distinctiveness is the combination of golf course with nature reserve which is something Lane has worked on for over ten years now. A 5.5km, 2-metre high fence was constructed to create a predator-free environment for fallow deer and other species. The fence not only has a sharp angle at the top to prevent animals climbing in but it also goes underground to prevent others from burrowing. Of course, before building this they had to remove the existing predators (stoats, weasels, possums etc.) from inside. Wairekei also has a creche for Kiwi chicks and a retirement home for retired breeding Takahē, another of New Zealand's rare native birds. I am not a bird expert but increasingly enjoy trying to identify wild birdlife that I see on golf courses. New Zealand has a huge number of distinctive native birds. I never saw a kiwi in the wild but I did in the course of my travels clock up a tui, numerous pukeko, a kea and was pointed out a pair of Weiweia which I was told was quite a rare siting.

Wairekei is difficult to characterise as a golf course. It is unashamedly parkland though in the hot, dry conditions I played it, there was plenty of bounce and roll. There are many good distinctive holes with plenty of variety, especially during the middle holes of the two loops of nine where the biggest elevation changes happen. But the overall impression of the course is its beauty and peacefulness. I remember thinking that it looked like Augusta. I have not been to Augusta, never mind played it, so I can only make an imaginary comparison but since having that thought, I have read a review which called it 'New Zealand's Augusta' so I think it is a legitimate comparison. The fairways and greens are immaculate; there are flowering shrubs framing some of the greens; there are quaint arched stone bridges over trickling streams. I've discussed before whether courses with glorious views sometime flatter the quality of a golf course. Here the views are not far reaching as you are encased in a wooded parkland with just glimpses of longer vistas but I think the reverse might be true. Somehow the quality of the golf course seems incidental to the enjoyment of the captivating ambience of the place.

There are streams and small ponds which act as water hazards but they are never too intrusive. This makes sense and I am not a fan of too much water on a golf course and I have previously quoted Peter Thomson himself regarding some water hazards as contrived. Here they sit naturally within the environment and are never the central feature of a hole's design. Some of the best holes are the shorter par 4s; the dog-leg 8th and 11 and 12 which all require good placement off the tee rather than just blasting it as far as possible. The two best par 3 are probably 5 which with its fairly wide but not very deep green with shrubs at the back and the creek at the front has shades of the 12th at Augusta and 15, a longer hole, playing downhill which reminded me of 14th at St George's Hill. The most memorable Par 5 is the 14th which has a tight tee shot and climbs up to a green perched on a ridge where even a short third shot feels hazardous.

What was remarkable about playing Wairekei was that the course had suffered badly from Cyclone Gabrielle twelve months previously. The estate had lost between 1,500 and 2,000 trees and the sanctuary fence had been extensively damaged which of course had upset the wildlife predator protection. Such is the scale of the place I really didn't notice the loss of trees less than a year after the event. Clearly much repair work had been done, a credit to all involved.

Parkland golf courses have not perhaps had their fair share of representation in *Of Peats and Putts*. I ended my second book on Scotland with a visit to the Roxburghe in the Scottish Borders and was perhaps a little ambivalent about it. Again, there can be much debate about what is a 'parkland' course as opposed to a 'heathland' or a 'moorland'. It is really more about the turf and the grasses and most importantly how the course plays. Sandy soil and fine grasses which enable the ball to bounce and which encourages bump-and-run golf as opposed to target golf is what matters as opposed to any particular definition. Obviously, the locality and weather conditions affect a course's characteristics, its 'terroir' to use a whisky expression stolen from the wine industry. Many 'heathland' courses in the U.K. get very wet in winter. I played Wairekei in the height of the New Zealand summer and it played enjoyably – I can't vouch for how it plays in a wet New Zealand winter.

Pokeno whisky matures quickly given its unusual climate

Te Arai - pine trees and lots of sand

CHAPTER 16

AUCKLAND

AFTER NEARLY A week on the North Island, I was feeling a lack of whisky and for this I had to head north. Auckland is by far and away the biggest city in New Zealand – over three times the population of the capital Wellington or Christchurch – and unlike other New Zealand cities, it feels like an international city. It was my first experience in New Zealand of traffic and the vibe of an international city. So, in some respects, Auckland is not typical New Zealand but in other respects it is important because it demonstrates that New Zealand is more than just a tourist destination. Also, if new golf courses or start-up whisky distilleries in New Zealand are going to attract international capital they will need an international financial centre like Auckland.

I didn't explore the city a lot but stayed down at the waterfront area which is the city's most distinctive area. There are some fine Victorian buildings around the harbour mingling with skyscrapers featuring the names of international corporate brands, as you would expect in an international city. My two destinations were both outside the city: Pōkeno Distillery, just under an hour to the south and Te Arai, just over an hour to the north.

Pōkeno is a town about fifty kilometres south of the centre of Auckland sitting in a valley just beyond the Bombay Hills which separate Auckland from the Waikato region. The enormous Waikato river flows nearby. It is New Zealand's largest river, meandering wildly through the upper half of the North Island from Lake Taupo to the sea about thirty kilometres west of Pokeno. It was a grey and misty morning as I drove there from Auckland and apparently this is not unusual as the climate is quite unique. The town sits below sea level and has misty mornings with high humidity, something which has a significant impact on whisky maturation. With the river and the surrounding volcanic hills, water supply is not a problem.

While I didn't explore it, the town is not particularly attractive and the distillery is a modern building on an industrial estate next to a large dairy factory – large dairy factories are quite common in New Zealand. The town is also renowned for Pokeno Bacon, a family business that has been producing high quality bacon and pork products for nearly fifty years. It can't be said that the immediate local environment is attractive but I understand the wider significance of the locality: the hills, the water and the climate. Perhaps I've been spoiled by visiting the likes of Waubs Harbour overlooking the coast, Cardrona sitting in the Crown Range mountains and Callington Mill in the historic town of Oatlands.

I had been introduced by Michael Fraser Milne to the owners and founders, Matt and Celine Johns and was shown around by Aaron, the Sales Manager. This is a distillery certainly inspired by the international success of Scotch whisky as Matt had many years' experience in the industry, most recently working for Tullirbardine in Perthshire. The upside of a green-field site on an industrial estate is the ability to design the process from scratch and the result is an impressive modern facility. There is space to double the existing capacity.

The business is focused on export and the proposition is a wider 'New Zealand' provenance more than a local 'Waikato/Pōkeno' one. The website unashamedly showcases New Zealand's dramatic landscapes across the whole country. With the exception of the stills which were sourced from McMillan of Prestonpans just outside Edinburgh, all the distillery equipment was designed and built in New Zealand and they use only New Zealand ingredients with the barley coming from Canterbury on the South Island. Experts believe that New Zealand malts have their own distinctive characteristics, more sweetness and a thicker texture which is ideal for Pōkeno wanting to create a distinctive New Zealand style. Gladfield Malt in Canterbury has now got a reputation for its quality internationally. Pōkeno has also experimented with other mash bills: chocolate roasted malt, toffee malt and manuka smoked malt. I remember the Holyrood Distillery in Edinburgh doing similar things.

Fermentation of eighty hours is relatively slow as is the distillation, all of which has been designed into the process. What is not slow is the maturation, a result of the unusual micro-climate which I had already experienced. With up to 97% humidity and high air pressure they find the bungs popping out of casks. This leads to an annual angel's share of up to 10% so long age statements are not going to be a feature although what they produce will be distinctive. The upside is that a business that was only founded in 2018 released its first products in 2022.

The other difference which Pōkeno has is its own cooperage, the only specialised whisky one in New Zealand. This allows them to repair and re-char barrels themselves as well as produce new barrels from native woods. Mike, the cooper, has created 200 litre barrels from totara wood, a native tree traditionally used for all sorts of items from wood carvings to weapons and food containers. The barrels are lightly toasted and charred and used to finish whisky that has been already matured in first-fill bourbon casks. This is part of their Exploration Series.

Pōkeno does offer tours on a Saturday but I sense this will not be an important part of the business. The industrial estate location and the distance from Auckland is not going to attract tourists in the numbers which they will get at the likes of Cardrona in the heart of the Queenstown holiday area. Instead, Pōkeno sees the potential on international markets for a New Zealand whisky proposition with the unusual fast maturation and on-site cooperage enabling them to experiment with different casks, giving them plenty of scope for producing high quality, distinctive products. As ever in the whisky market there are so many ways of being different. Pōkeno has a small and enthusiastic team with plenty of industry knowledge, a couple of interesting, distinctive approaches to making whisky, a state-of-the-art modern production facility and some good brand marketing, all of which should combine to give them success. I certainly wish them well.

The stretch of coastline at Te Arai is perfect for golf

I have said before that one of the many common characteristics of the golfing and whisky worlds is the common camaraderie of those involved and a willingness to share friends and connections. Just as Charles MacLean had introduced me to Michael Fraser Milne and Michael had steered me to Pōkeno, I had another amazing piece of luck which meant that the following day I was heading to Te Arai on the west coast north of Auckland. My previous books had drawn me into a friendship with Mark Horyna, a German writer and publisher with an enthusiasm for golf and Scottish golf in particular and he had asked me to contribute an article to a new European golf magazine which he was launching, *Depeche Golf*. When I told him that my next project was Tasmania and New Zealand he immediately introduced me to Andy Clements, an ex-Chairman of the New Zealand PGA. Andy gave me some advice on my itinerary, decided his own course at Whangamata was too much of a detour for me and instead arranged for us to play at Te Arai Links, the new golf resort about which I had been reading rave reviews. It was almost too good to be true.

The story of Te Arai must start with the development of Tara Iti, a Tom Doak designed course a few miles to the north which opened as a private club in 2015. The investment money came from an American billionaire, Rick Kayne with the development by John Darby, whose name we came across at Millbrook, Jack's Point and the new course at Wanaka. Such was the acclaim that Tara Iti was met with that Rick Kayne decided to build another resort just a few miles down the coast, where there are now two courses: Te Arai South, designed by Coore/Crenshaw, and Te Arai North designed again by Tom Doak. This time the development was undertaken by Jim Rohrstaff and the courses are open to the public. Most rankings of New Zealand golf courses now put Tara Iti and the two Te Arai courses all in the top three in the country.

All three are set on the same stretch of land and the first thing to say is that it is the perfect land for golf – seaside sandy soil amidst pine forests. I played Te Arai South so can't speak for the other two but I gather that while they all have some different characteristics, they share the fundamentals: a great location with delightful seaside views, perfect sandy turf with fescue grasses and the benefits of having a top designer plot the design and layout. As I came off the bitumen road onto a dirt track for the last few kilometres (I was used to this from Cape Wickham and I gather this is also the case at Tara Iti so I now know it is a good sign) I was bursting with anticipation. There are some golf courses where from a mile or two off, you just know that you are in for a treat.

Andy had arranged for us to play in a fourball with Greg Kenward, the General Manager of the resort and another member, Phil, so I was fortunate to be paying member's guest rate. While this is a high-end prestigious international golf resort, the atmosphere was relaxed and quite informal. The main clubhouse and bar/restaurant are based at the South Course, the latter, called Rick's Restaurant overlooking an enormous 2.5 acre (sic) putting green called the Playground. It's reminiscent of the Himalayas at St Andrew's. Indeed, it was probably inspired by it.

I was partnering Phil against Andy and Greg – I can't remember how that was decided upon but I will tell you now that we came second. The first hole is a long uphill Par 5 – it's quite a generously wide fairway as befits a first hole. My third shot to the green was not quite hard enough and ended up in sand just short of the green. I phrased that carefully because at the time I thought I was in a bunker – it looked like a bunker to me – but after playing out and looking around for a rake, I was told that there were no rakes as there were no bunkers because all sand was simply a waste area. You simply repaired the sand with your foot.

This was my first taste of the Te Arai golf philosophy which Greg was a strong exponent of. When playing at a top golf resort built with American money, I have a vision of things being formal and regimented. We were playing a fourball and I was prepared for the round to take four and a half hours. How wrong could I be? Greg's approach was to get on with it and not take things too seriously. If you find yourself in a hole where someone hasn't properly repaired the sand you just move it, gimmes were on the generous side (fretting over short putts isn't really fun and golf should be fun) and ready golf was the order of the day. I even think we were allowed one Mulligan each. We were round in nearer three hours than four; that's my kind of golf!

In fact, I think this was the one round where I might have preferred to have played more slowly as I was wanting to take in not only the gorgeous views but also the design of the holes and savour the whole experience. I didn't have time to take extensive notes on the holes which I would have if I had been playing on my own. But Greg was adamant that slow play was anathema to the resort's philosophy and that guests would be encouraged to play at a good pace. Very refreshing.

I cannot therefore describe every individual hole because I can't remember them all. What I can describe is an overall impression of the type of golf Te Arai encourages. The comparison with Barnbougle is obvious as next door to each other are two great links courses, one designed by Tom Doak and one by Coore and Crenshaw. Te Arai South, being the Coore Crenshaw creation, is therefore the Lost Farm of Te Arai but I think the design philosophy has moved on even further. I gather that the grass-seed mix for the fairways and greens was the same except for a higher concentration being used on the greens. Certainly, you could use your putter from a long way out and often, with the exaggerated contours, it was the best option. What is important is that you have a choice – that is what to me makes a great golf course. There is more than one way of getting the ball to the hole.

Te Arai South boasts '16 ocean view' holes. By contrast I believe that Te Arai North is a little more varied with more inland holes amongst the pine trees. It is generally regarded as the greater test of the two. What I remember is a wonderful variety of holes – there are 4 Par 5s and 4 Par 3s – and it is not long, under 6,000 yards off the main tees, about 6,400 yards off the visitor back tees. There are some great short par 4s – four of the Par 4s are under 350 yards but they are not easy holes. The 16th is just over 300 yards off the visitor tees but is stroke index 8 for a reason. Nor is the Par 3 17th, just 110 yards, easy, as its stroke index of 14 suggests. Sitting alongside the sea it is exposed to whatever wind there is and the entrance to the green is very narrow. Greg said that in some wind conditions a putter was definitely the best option off the tee. I was reminded of the Par 3 15th at Gullane No. 3 where I always take a putter and when, the last time I played it, I got my '3 putt Par at a Par 3'. Te Arai is a 'classic' modern links where the challenge lies not in length nor penal rough and bunkers but in the natural variability of the terrain and the weather conditions, the wind in particular. With the first 9 lying to the south of the clubhouse and the back 9 to the north, you get holes going in all directions and, as at Cape Wickham, you get the sea to your right as well as the sea to your left; if you have mastered the right to left wind off the sea on holes 6-9 then you need to master a left to right wind off the sea on holes 15-18.

Not only was Greg's speed of play impressive, his golf game was remarkable. From early on, many of his tee shots headed off wildly into the many waste areas. Somehow, however, he would appear back on the green where he would single putt and make par. This happened on a regular basis much to the consternation of my partner Phil and me. So together with Andy's steadier play we were always up against it. Arguably the course did not punish Greg's waywardness enough but, as ever, a good short game can make up for deficiencies off the tee as Seve used to prove. Yes, I think 'Seve-esque' would be a good description of Greg's game that day.

After the game we had a quick drink and a sandwich in Rik's Restaurant and Greg talked about the developments – the smart houses being built around the course and the new restaurant. Te Arai will be a mixture of a member's club and a pay and play – green fees, I fear will be high but you will certainly be treated royally in every respect. I wonder also to what extent the building of houses around the courses will affect the ambience though it won't be intensive. The courses are built on an enormous stretch of land and there is plenty of room.

As I headed back along the dirt track to the main road, I reflected on a day which had passed in a blur. Waking up in downtown Auckland seemed an age away. Links golf in remote locations has that effect – I wished that I could have slowed down the whole day to savour the experience even more. I hoped that one day I could come back for more.

The great Par 5 11th hole at Waitangi

The perilous short Par 4 16th at Kauri Cliffs

CHAPTER 17

NORTHLAND
AND THE BAY
OF ISLANDS

IT'S ANOTHER DECISION when visiting New Zealand whether to venture north from Auckland into Northland and the Bay of Islands area. It's six-hundred kilometres from Paraparaumu beach to Auckland; it's another 400 from Auckland to Cape Reinga at the tip of the North Island. You wouldn't venture here for whisky – I found no evidence of any distilleries – but there are plenty of golfing options. The most northerly is probably the Carrington Estate on the Karikari peninsula north of Doubtless Bay where in 2003 a resort course was built by Matt Dye, nephew of the famous Pete Dye. It is, by all accounts, a very scenic spot, but I had read that the quality of the course had suffered in recent years and it is a long way to get there. I was, however, keen to go to Ahipara, almost as far north on the west coast, where I had read about a links course. My drive from Te Arai was not without its challenges. Having found my way back onto State Highway 1, which is the main route north, I found that there was a diversion due to significant roadworks. While in the UK, a diversion off a main highway might be a few miles – it might even cost you twenty-to-thirty minutes –in New Zealand, diversions, like the landscape and scenery, are on a different scale. The diversion must have been some fifty kilometres as it took me back to the east coast which was a little unfortunate as I was heading for the west coast. To this day I do not know whether, if I had ignored the diversion signs and persevered, I could have cut across to where I was going. I made it by dusk to Hokianga Harbour, a charmingly beautiful and tranquil river estuary sprinkled with small islands and overlooked by ancient forests of native kauri trees. It felt a million miles away from the bustle of Auckland which I had left that morning. After a relaxing breakfast the following morning overlooking the wide estuary and a clifftop walk with the mouth of the estuary on one side and the Tasman Sea on the other, I drove a short distance inland to take the small ferry from Raweme to Kohukohu on the other side. To drive around the end of the estuary would have taken 1½ hours so this fifteen-minute service makes sense. You can tell from the names that this area is rich in Māori history and there is much to do and see in the area.

I headed further north and eventually hit the coast again at Ahipara which is a small settlement at the start of the famous 90-Mile Beach. 90-Mile Beach is the west side of the small pointy bit at the top of the slightly bigger small pointy bit of New Zealand north of Auckland. I would have loved to have gone further and got to Cape Reinga but, as the name suggests, it is ninety miles there and ninety miles back so I would have needed more time than I had.

The golf course occupies the coast for the first of the ninety miles. It used to be called Kaitaia Golf Club after the slightly bigger town some fifteen kilometres inland but has recently been re-branded 90 Mile Beach Golf Links. I can see the thinking in attracting the likes of me as a visitor. Unfortunately, I arrived on a day when the course was closed for maintenance. I would probably only have had time for 9 holes in any case so instead I walked around. It's a classic spot for a links-style course, set right against the beach though in parts sheltered behind some dunes. The fairways are delightfully rumpled and sometimes forming pleasing valleys, while many of the tee boxes are raised giving views of both the challenge ahead and the beach and coastline. The other interesting feature of the course was the number Norfolk pine trees. You don't usually associate links courses with trees but these tall, elegant and distinctively shaped trees certainly add character to the environment and at times help shape the course. I left with a sense of frustration at not being able to swing a club.

I was staying over on the east coast at Russell in the Bay of Islands. If there is a tourist centre for Northland, this is it and it is a very pretty spot. Nearby are the famous Waitangi Treaty Grounds. I had planned a couple of days here and had two golf courses in my sights; Waitangi itself alongside the Treaty Grounds and Kauri Cliffs which I had decided to play. Russell is a picturesque town with charming colonial architecture. It is reached via a small car ferry from Opua just along the coast from Paihia, the main town and Waitangi itself. Russell is not on an island but a long peninsula, the ten-minute ferry journey saving a drive of over an hour. Russell is small, perhaps more a village than a town, with a prosperous feel. There are many shops and along the seafront, small hotels and restaurants. My bed and breakfast was set up on a hill at the back of the village with a fine view from my balcony across the bay. A small passenger ferry also runs across the bay to Pahia allowing you to choose restaurants on either side of the bay.

Kauri Cliffs is about fifty kilometres up the coast from Waitangi and was the first of the two resort courses built in New Zealand by the American Hedge Fund manager, Julian Robertson. Kauri Cliffs dates from 1999 with Cape Kidnappers following about five years later. The resorts are all about the location, dramatic clifftop settings with extensive coastal views. Unlike Te Arai where the terrain is perfect for a golf course and the views are a bonus, here a golf course has been created to make the most of the views. The estate size is some 4,500 acres so there was plenty of room. I can't make comparisons with Cape Kidnappers because I didn't play there and you can't just roll up to have a mooch around at these courses as I did at 90 Mile Beach – the estates are gated and you are met with an intercom several kilometres from the clubhouse.

These resorts are exclusive in that they are expensive but they are open for those who pay the, in the view of many, exorbitant green fees. While I see the escalating cost of green fees internationally as regrettable, if it is what the market can bear then, I don't see what the problem is. As I mentioned earlier, in Australia and New Zealand there is a two-tier system whereby international visitors are charged the full fee and the cost for New Zealand residents is significantly less. I have no problem with this as when I am visiting a country, I am actually happy to pay more for a green fee than I am in my own country. I have noticed that this approach is starting to become more common in Scotland, where demand from America has pushed up green fees and put them out of reach of many domestic golfers. I believe that the market for members of UK golf clubs is different so a lower green fee level is appropriate.

The approach to Kauri Cliffs was by the now familiar dirt track and having been allowed through the estate gates via the intercom I was met in the car park and escorted to the clubhouse on a golf buggy. It is expensive but a strong service culture was evident – it was clear that they were expecting 'Mr Brown' and that they would look after him. I had arrived early – I wanted to get my money's worth - and was told that the golf course was not busy and that I could go out whenever I wanted to. 'Not busy' was a bit of an understatement. I couldn't see any other golfers apart from one on the practice range. I subsequently met another group on the 8th who let me through immediately. Otherwise, I had the course to myself which was slightly surreal.

The Norfolk pines give a distinctive look to 90 Mile Beach Golf links at Ahipara

Let's start with the views – they are magnificent and far-reaching. It was a pleasant afternoon though not quite crystal clear, but you could see both ways along the coast of the enormous Takou Bay. The lodge and clubhouse are situated on the highest bit of land and you do feel on top of the world, but it is a very different sensation from a seaside links such as Te Arai and Barnbougle or even the clifftop/ links mix of Cape Wickham or The New South Wales. The sea is a dramatic backdrop but doesn't really feel part of the course.

The first hole starts inland behind the lodge and the first few holes are quite a distance from the coast though with the elevation you still have the long views. There is nothing particularly special about the first four holes. The short 5th and the 6th are both more dramatic, the latter requiring a brave drive over a deep valley. You only really experience the sea, or rather the cliffs, at the short 7th on the front 9 where the green is attractively situated against the backdrop of the ocean and there is plenty of terrifying trouble to your right. 8 and 9 then take you back inland towards the clubhouse, the latter strongly uphill.

The first 4 holes of the back 9, 10-13 are all away from the sea and on a lower level so you have a rest from the views. The holes are actually quite interesting: a short downhill Par 4, a longer Par 4 with the green surrounded by marshland, a strong uphill Par 3 and a pleasing sloped dogleg Par 4 as you climb back up to the coast. Holes 14-17 are then what you came for. They all head back south along the coast and hug the top of the cliffs in sometimes dramatic fashion. Every shot you take has this context. 14 is a long downhill Par 3 which feels a little scary. My drive at the Par 5 15th was almost too brave as it ended about a foot from the edge of the cliff and I just had room for a stance to hit my second safely inland, despite the hole doglegging back to the left for the third shot. I didn't learn my lesson as my drive at the short Par 4 16th was also slightly too far left and here you have to hope that you catch one of the five bunkers because if you don't, you won't see your ball again. I played a second ball down the middle this time. The second shot to the small green is sharply down hill with the top of the cliff lurking menacingly behind. 17 is a slightly longer, slightly less scary version of 16 before at 18 you again drive over one of Kauri's huge ravines and back up to the clubhouse.

I hugely enjoyed my afternoon. But this is parkland golf with dramatic sea views; it is not, in my sense of the expression, 'seaside golf' but 'golf by the sea'. As an example, the 16th is an excellent short Par 4; if you are accurate off the tee, it is likely to be a short wedge into the small green. But there is some long grass short of the green, so there is really only one shot option. Decide what club and how hard to hit it and hope it lands and stops. There is no bump and run option which you would have on a links or a dry heathland. Generally, I felt the course was a parkland design with few run-off areas. I'm not saying it is a bad design but it is not my type of course or design. I am delighted to have played it but don't yearn to go back. Te Arai by contrast, I would love to play again.

I played Waitangi the following day for about a tenth of the price – yes, it was a lot more expensive than Hokitika! In the morning, I went to the Treaty Grounds. This was the site of the famous treaty signed in 1840 between the British Crown colony and the Māori chiefs which is recognised as New Zealand's founding document as it agreed how the country would be governed, giving sovereignty to the British government while protecting Māori rights. The treaty was signed in both English and Māori (something which has made its exact interpretation difficult to define) and taken around the country to be signed by some five hundred Māori chiefs. It remains controversial to this day as many say that Māori rights have not been upheld and in 1975 the Waitangi Tribunal was set up to determine exact meaning and investigate alleged treaty breeches. Today there is a museum and you can walk around the grounds, visit the home of the Governor General and learn about Māori culture. It is impressively organised.

With hindsight, it was a mistake to have played Waitangi on a warm Saturday afternoon but this had been dictated by availability at

Kauri Cliffs. I had played all over New Zealand and not experienced one busy golf course but that afternoon, play was disappointingly slow. It does, however, allow me to make my normal rant about slow play. I think I am like most people and think that other road drivers generally either drive too fast or too slowly. It's the same with other golfers, except with golfers it is the slow ones who are the more annoying. I still cannot understand how golf keeps getting slower though I think it starts with the professional game. Amateurs then tend to copy the professionals: needing to know the exact distance, taking an age to assess the wind and worrying too much as to whether it is a six iron or a seven iron. For a professional this is quite important but to most amateurs there are so many more variables that the right club is often the least of their problems! I do think that many amateurs would enjoy golf more if they just worried a little less and used their instinct a bit more.

The issue is not confined to golf. Cricket has become much slower. The solution to this was to invent a shortened form of the game, 20/20 cricket, but ironically this is played even more slowly than Test cricket. Originally designed to take about three hours, it now routinely takes much longer. Indeed, I think the problem with 20/20 cricket is that it is too long for television – who wants to sit down and watch something for more than three hours? With Test cricket you can dip in and out at any time. Golf seems to be experimenting with something in America which seems to me to be so far away from proper golf that it is meaningless. Instead, I would suggest a return to hickory golf which I have recently started to play. Just maybe six clubs in your pencil bag, no need for a trolley and all the faff of remembering to charge your battery, no distance devices to worry about, just envisage the shot and swing. It frees the mind incredibly as you don't worry about exact yardages and club selection

– it so much more liberating. I recently played eighteen holes of it in a fourball in under three hours. I will write more about this in future books.

Here I enjoy the contrast with trends in whisky. In most industries, the motivation is to make things more quickly and efficiently. The boom in malt whisky has come from some start-ups making whisky more slowly by experimenting with various parts of the process whether it be slower fermentation, slower distilling, triple distilling or longer maturation. The urge is for something different not something cheaper.

There was a bit of a buzz about the club at Waitangi as the previous week, the new professional had just won the New Zealand PGA Tournament at Hastings by completing his final four holes in birdie, birdie, eagle, birdie! He was ambling around the clubhouse with a big smile on his face. Fortunately, it was a lovely day and so I didn't worry much about the slow play and it gave me time to savour the lovely views on the back 9. I offered to join up with a Japanese couple behind me but despite lots of smiles, they declined – or maybe there was a bit of a language barrier. The front 9 is inland amongst woods and is largely unremarkable, though there is a testing drive through a gap in the trees at 5 and an excellent Par 3 at 6. The back 9 is mainly on the hill facing the bay with the Par 5 11th by some distance the best hole on the course as it wends its way towards the sea, its sloping fairway narrowing all the way down to an extremely pretty green at the water's edge. It is testing golf and a very pretty hole. You then traverse up and down the hill before walking back across the road at the top for a strong downhill Par 3 at 16 while 17 and 18 are both interesting dog-legs to finish. It is an enjoyable golf course in a very pleasant environment, though perhaps no more than that. I was perhaps left with the feeling that 90 Mile Beach golf course had been my favourite in the area and I hadn't even played it.

Waiheke Golf Club is set in a pretty valley

The distinctive stills at Waiheke Whisky

CHAPTER 18

WAIHEKE ISLAND

I HAVE LEFT the best to last. I have spoken of the need to make choices when visiting New Zealand as there is so much to see, and for many Waiheke Island is unlikely to make the cut. It is a 45-minute ferry journey from Auckland so requires a full day to visit. Most tourists will probably explore the city itself, go up the Sky Tower, take a harbour cruise or perhaps go further afield and visit the much larger Coromandel Peninsula. Waiheke is a charmingly quiet island much favoured by Auckland commuters as a haven from the city's bustle, though in the height of summer it attracts many local day trippers. It has a golf course but not one that would appear in the country's list of the top 100. It was probably always going to be on my itinerary as it was here that one of the first of the new wave of New Zealand whisky distilleries was conceived back in 2010. But serendipity continued to stalk me – I had not known that both golf and whisky in Tasmania had begun in Bothwell – and to discover that the one person I wanted to visit in the whole of New Zealand lived on Waiheke Island and was an ex-President of the Golf Club which sits just across the road – a 9 iron with the wind behind – from the new site of Waiheke Whisky was just too good to be true.

Let me explain. In May 2018, I published my first book, *Of Peats and Putts*. It was an exciting time for me as any first-time author seeing their book in print will understand. Many friends kindly bought copies – some who clearly never had any intention of reading them – and I was encouraged by the response. On 15th June, I received an email from Tom Hepburn which started 'Hello Andrew, from Waiheke Island, New Zealand (yes, it's on the map!).' I did indeed look it up on a map. He had read about my book in the excellent *Golf Quarterly* publication where I had been fortunate to receive a generous review and I was delighted that my reach now included the southern hemisphere. Tom explained that he was a Scot who enjoyed golf and single malts 'particularly the Islay variety'. He was clearly in my target market. What was more remarkable was that he had been born in Galashiels in the Scottish Borders, four miles from my family home and where my father had grown up. So started a regular email correspondence and I determined that one day I would visit Waiheke Island.

After an early breakfast in my small apartment on the Auckland waterfront, I joined the queue for the Waiheke Ferry. It is quite a busy commuter route but I was surprised that there were also many passengers heading out to Waiheke in the morning. There are many islands off the coast of Auckland in what is a relatively sheltered bay with Auckland to the west and the Firth of Thames and the Coromandel peninsula to the east. Waiheke is the largest of these and now has a population of nearly 10,000. Great Barrier Island is larger but lies some way off the coast and has only one tenth the population. It was a pleasant ferry journey and a good way of seeing Auckland's waterfront buildings. As it chugged further away, I felt that I could have been on a Caledonian McBrayne on the Firth of Clyde. It had been nearly six years since the email from Tom so I was genuinely excited at the prospect of meeting him – we had even exchanged 'selfies' to ensure we recognised each other.

I had left all the arrangements to Tom and he didn't disappoint: golf in the morning, lunch at a well-known vineyard followed by an afternoon visit to the distillery and a short trip round the sights of the island.

We started with golf or rather a coffee in the clubhouse with Tom and his friend Eric, better known as 'Woody'. Woody also claimed Scottish ancestry, indeed he was from a family of Scottish 'Browns' who had emigrated in the 1870s. The clubhouse can best be described as functional but it is pleasantly located, overlooking the course with a veranda outside and attractive shrubs separating it from the car park. Inside was everything you would expect in a small golf clubhouse – I enjoyed seeing a photograph of the President from 1987/88, one Tom Hepburn. The club dates from 1961 and the course has been in its current location in a pretty valley off Onetangi Road near the centre of the island since 1973. The plan was always for it to become eighteen holes but there have been endless long disputes about the lease which I gather have not yet been resolved so today it remains essentially a 9 hole course with 18 tee boxes and 11 greens. It's even more complicated than King Island – on the back 9 the 2nd (11th) is replaced by the 13th while the 4th and 12th play from different tee boxes to nearby greens along virtually the same fairway. Anyway, this didn't concern me as we restricted ourselves to 9 holes; we had other important matters to attend to, namely lunch and the visit to the whisky distillery.

After coffee and a lot of familiar golfing banter, we set off down the Par 5 1st hole. Tom had recently recovered from an illness so this was his first golf for a while. He started cautiously but soon the muscle memory kicked in and what clearly had been a more than useful swing was evident. It was a pleasant morning and it is a very pleasant place to play golf. There is quite a lot of water on the course and it was obvious that it could get wet in winter. A lake to the left of the 1st is not really a factor but a network of streams (we Scots would call then burns) do very much come into play at 6,7 and 8. My favourite holes were the Par 4s at 4 and 6, the former a dog-leg, the latter also a dog-leg requiring a well-placed drive over a swamp, and the Par 3 8th which requires a confident strike across a pond and then over an inlet from the sea. The other notable feature of the first 9 holes is something which I don't think I noticed at the time. Waiheke shares a distinction with the Old Course at St Andrews. It has a palindromic Par pattern – 1 and 9 are Par 5s, 2 and 8 Par 3s and the others in the middle are Par 4s. Of course, St Andrews manages this over 18 holes which is much more difficult and to this day no one has managed to contradict my contention that the Old Course is the only course in the world to achieve this. Surely there must be one somewhere?

I'm not sure who won our threeball but I am sure that none of us cared too much. We headed off fairly quickly to Stonyridge Vineyard which is located just across the road from the golf course – yes, the course neighbours both a vineyard and a whisky distillery, surely another unique distinction.

In fact, there are four vineyards within a few hundred yards. Stonyridge is a beautiful place with ivy-clad buildings and a restaurant and terrace at the back overlooking gentle slopes of vines. Woody was a VIP member so we were given special treatment, with him insisting that we should taste some of their special wines. The Stonyridge Larose vintages sell for several hundred NZ $ and are considered to be some of the top red wines in New Zealand, a match for the best Bordeaux can offer. Also delicious was the lamb we ate – the best I had had in all of New Zealand.

I'm not sure whether this was the ideal preparation for a whisky distillery visit but needs must and we travelled the few hundred yards east to the distillery. In fact, wine does play a role at Waiheke because the current distiller, Patrick Newton, was an award-winning wine maker at one of the other vineyards on the island, Mudbrick. Waiheke Whisky has been operating slightly under the radar for over a decade but has recently come to prominence with its move to a new site, the winning of a number of awards and a very active social media presence.

TOM HEPBURN
PRESIDENT
1987-1988

Waiheke Club President 1987-1988

The business had been founded in 2010 by Mark Izzard and Richard Evert operating from a small shed on the island and continued for a number of years on a fairly small scale. Today's new site for the distillery is a joint site with Waiheke Brewing Co. which also started on a small scale, indeed at one point in the very same shed. Bringing the businesses together to operate from the same site, and including all the hospitality which goes with it, makes obvious sense. The site is called 'The Heke' - *heke* is a Māori word meaning to 'ebb, drip or trickle' which seems to fit well with whisky. As well as offering brewery and distillery visits and tastings, the site includes a restaurant, several bars, extensive gardens with Māori sculptures and even two golf simulator bays! The owners are also classic car enthusiasts so you will spot the odd, interesting exhibit. The whole place has a relaxed and friendly vibe about it which extends to Mac the dog in the Boilermaker Bar. That's now two dogs I have met in a whisky distillery.

We were met by Mark and Roanne Izzard who treated us royally and seemed delighted that I had brought my two minders, Tom and Woody, with me. We were given a tasting where Mark outlined his approach – there was much discussion about peat with Tom expressing his love of Islay malts – and then a trip around the distillery where the famous geodesic spirit still was very much star of the show. I am not sure that I, a historian, am the best person to explain either what a geodesic still is or the science behind why it makes a difference but I will try. The original small still which they used before moving to the new distillery was designed by their engineer, Eric, to be geodesic to maximise the volume-to-surface area and the amount of vertical reflux. The stills were called VITRIOL 1 and 2 after the motto of a 15th-century alchemist Basilius Valentinus; '*Visita Interiora Terrae Rectificando Invenies Occultum Lapidem*'. This, as most of my readers will obviously know, translates as *"Visit the interior of the earth and purifying you will find the hidden stone"*. I promise you I am not making this up – you can read more about it on their website.

Geodesic, as I understand, is a dome shape comprising twenty equilateral triangles. When they scaled up for the new distillery, they worked with Speyside Copper Works and asked for a similar design, a challenge which Speyside Copper Works took up and delivered. Apparently, the result is more icosahedronic rather than geodesic – please don't ask me to explain the difference. What I can say is that it is a handsome-looking object and as ever with a new whisky business is important in giving them an 'angle' to promote their uniqueness.

Another innovation has been to use screw tops. Their argument is one of sustainability dispensing with the importing of sometimes unreliable cork from Portugal plus the greater recyclability of screw-top materials. New Zealand of course was one of the first countries to bring screw tops into the wine industry and they are not alone in whisky as the Japanese have been using screw tops for some time.

The other two areas of focus for the business are the maturation and peat. Being on an island known mainly for quality wines gives them some interesting options on barrels, especially with the contacts in the industry which Patrick Newton brings. There are over thirty vineyards on Waiheke growing a wide range of grape varieties so there is a ready stock of used barrels available. They also do their own re-toasting and re-charring of barrels.

They have been interested in peat for a number of years and in emphasising the different type of flavour imparted by New Zealand peat. Peat from Islay is largely marine vegetation with sea salt giving iodine, tar and seaweed flavours. New Zealand peat comes largely from the Invercargill area on the South Island and is predominantly wetland and bog based, composed of sphagnum moss, wire rush, sedges and flax. There is little wood in the peat which makes it less 'smoky' and you don't get the 'iodine/antiseptic' notes you sometimes get with the stronger Islay whiskies. The effect is generally described as being more 'gentle'; Waiheke refer to their main peat expression, called 'Moss', as having a 'resinous, liquorice quality'. Waiheke seems to be the only New Zealand whisky which is exploring this real difference in some depth. I'd be surprised if Auld Farm Distillery which sits in the heart of the area where the peat comes from doesn't experiment with this too.

I was delighted to learn since my visit that Waiheke gained recognition at the 2025 World Whisky Awards with its DYAD Peat + Port expression named Category Winner for Small Batch Single Malt (twelve years & under). It's other entry, a limited edition non-peated aged in three different casks called 'Cantankerous' also received a Gold Medal in its category. 'Cantankerous' is dedicated to the late writer Iain Banks who wrote one of the great books on whisky, *Raw Spirit*. Banks, as Iain M Banks, also wrote the *Culture* series of science fiction stories which included a starship named Cantankerous. Waiheke had previously won awards in New Zealand but this international recognition will stand the business in good stead as it builds its export business.

Finally, it is worth mentioning that Waiheke has used social media actively – I think Roanne has been behind much of this. I am certainly no expert on social media – my marketing skills belong to an age which pre-dates it – but I found Waiheke much more active and prominent than its other New Zealand competitors, or indeed those I had visited in Tasmania. There is no doubt that for a start-up business in a niche market, social media is very important. Indeed, the existence of social media with its ability to target cost effectively small groups of interested consumers has helped small start-up whisky businesses all over the world and has been a contributory factor to their success.

There was just time for Tom to take me on a short drive around the island, in particular the attractive beach front on Onetangi Bay where he pointed out some of his and Woody's favourite restaurants, before heading back to the ferry terminal to say our good-byes.

I was nearing the end of my New Zealand adventure. I had visited Milford Sound and flown in a small plane across the Southern Alps. I had enjoyed the wonders of Wanaka, driven up the west coast of the South Island through the dramatic glacier country, seeing the magical reflection of Mounts Cook and Tasman on Lake Matheson. Then in the North Island, I had marvelled at the volcanic eruptions around Taupo and Rotorua and the delightful scenery of the Bay of Islands. I had played some wonderful golf courses in some glorious locations from Jack's Point and Arrowtown in the South Island to Paraparaumu Beach and Te Arai (to name but a few) in the North Island. But this had been my favourite day of all. It had all the elements. Starting with a ferry ride, the day got off to a perfect start and what followed had everything I could have hoped for. I don't mind playing golf courses alone but to play a three ball with Tom and Woody was very special. By the end it was as if we had known each other for years. There followed an excellent lunch and excellent lunches are a critical requirement of any perfect golfing day – more so than an excellent dinner, I would suggest. Then as a digestif, to be entertained at an impressive new whisky distillery in such a relaxed manner by Mark and his team (another mention here for Mac the dog who was the most relaxed of them all) was the perfect conclusion – or not quite the conclusion as I had the return ferry journey to enjoy as well.

Whisky and golf, that somewhat contrived pairing I had conjured up nearly a decade ago, have so much in common and Waiheke Island had delivered everything I love about each of them: friendships, fun and learning. Golf is always best enjoyed when playing with like-minded people and I make no apology for repeating the description coined many years ago that the best golf should be 'serious fun'. The same is true of whisky – it is best enjoyed with others and accompanied by banter, but banter based on beliefs in this and that. And learning is why I write these books – there is always more to learn about golf, about whisky, about yourself. Every golf course has its own history, every round you play has its own distinction and every whisky distillery has its own character - there are no geodesic stills in Scotland. I stood on the deck of the ferry looking out over Auckland harbour, the freshening wind providing a pleasant chill to my face, concluding that the previous eight hours had enriched my life and provided a fitting conclusion to an enriching eight weeks. What more could I ask for?

AFTERWORD

I HAVE PREVIOUSLY compared life to a round of golf as it delivers good moments and bad moments, slices of fortune and bouts of misfortune and, whatever your expectations, nearly always something which takes you by surprise. In golf, as in life, managing to keep the good and the bad in perspective and dealing with the unforeseen is how you will prosper.

At the time, I said that if I hoped to live for four score years and ten, I was about to putt out on the 12th green. Now, a further six years down the line, I am teeing it up on the 14th, nearly halfway through the back nine. How time flies when you are enjoying yourself.

It might be convenient for my purposes if, six years on, I conclude this book with some radical new insights into whisky and golf which my extensive travels through Tasmania and New Zealand have given me, some revelations or some new understanding which leads me to reappraise or at least refine some of my previous hypotheses. Try as I may, I can't find any. In fact, what I have witnessed and enjoyed has merely served to reaffirm most of my previous views and prejudices. I find that reassuring.

I talked in *Of Peats and Putts Continental,* where I visited nine European countries, about how struck I was by the universality of the core values of whisky and golf, how enthusiasts for each can quickly relate to each other and despite any language barriers soon engage positively in discussing the same issues. The whisky enthusiasts with views on the likes of peat or sherry casks and the golfers expounding the glories of a particular course they have played. This has been the case wherever I travelled during the research for this book. The 'issues' are generally the same though sometimes with a local twist. In whisky there is an enormous respect for the history and values of Scotch whisky but a desire to add some distinctive feature and, increasingly, to produce not just malt whisky produced in Australia or New Zealand but to produce Australian and New Zealand whisky. With golf, there is a recognition and understanding of the history of the game, often relating back to Scotland but also embracing new design trends – most of the new developments focusing on the landscape and the turf.

Whisky is a very new industry in each country but is already beginning to show an incredible diversity of offerings and business models: ownerships ranging from multi-nationals down to small family businesses and large differences in scale just as you will see in Scotland. The challenge for the industry will be its ability to export as the explosion in capacity is unlikely to be matched by an increase in local demand and the key to successful export will be quality. Obviously, the early pioneers were inspired by Scotland but some Australian distilleries had a reputation for being somewhat simplistic – distilling wort from a local brewery and relying on fortified wine casks to deliver quick flavour. Indeed, experts at one time compared this to the Australian wine industry which, for a while, had a reputation for producing unsubtle 'over-oaked' products. The operators I met understood that this was not going to be a sustainable way forward and now there is a great deal of focus on the distilling and maturation processes, combined with exploration of and experimentation with the likes of heritage barleys, different yeasts, local peat as well as a range of cask types.

Sustainability is recognised as an important factor and most of the new businesses have built this into their process and almost all distilleries identify strongly with their locality. This latter point is so fundamental to whisky; as the title of Dave Broom's recent book suggests, it has and needs *A Sense of Place*. It is therefore not surprising that Callington Mill calls itself 'Tasmanian Whisky', Hellyers Road on its new design has 'North West Tasmania' and Waubs Harbour is 'Tasmanian Maritime Whisky'. With many fewer distilleries in New Zealand most brands focus on being just 'New Zealand Whisky' but I notice Reefton on their website calling themselves 'West Coast – New Zealand'.

The role of tourism in the business model is also similar to the many start-ups in Scotland and Ireland with Australia and New Zealand copying the 'Cellar Door' concept from their wine trade. My final day on Waiheke probably summed up the tourism opportunity: golf in the morning, lunch and wine tasting at a vineyard followed by an afternoon distillery visit. All you need is two drivers, one in your golf bag and one to take you back to where you are staying!

In golf the new courses being built are largely 'super-premium' elite venues targeting an international market where 'destination' golfers look to 'tick off' another bucket list course. This is producing some wonderful golf courses built by some of the world's top designers in dramatic locations and increasingly, like Te Arai, on land perfect for golf. The good thing about these courses is that they are rediscovering the important elements of great golf which start with the turf. Golf courses, like whisky brands, need 'a sense of place' but this should not be confined to great scenery but also to the fundamentals of the land on which it is built, the golf course's 'terroir' if you like. That is why I preferred Te Arai to Kauri Cliffs – the choice of location for the latter was driven by the scenery alone while with the former it was the terrain.

The big downside of these new developments is that they are creating a completely separate market for visiting golfers with green fees at these venues escalating dramatically –£400+ is not uncommon – so they are out of reach for many. But to enjoy golf, the 'serious fun', which is the essence of proper golf, you don't need to go to a Top 10 or Top 100 course and pay a £400 green fee. We all have a price we are prepared to pay but both Tasmania and New Zealand offer plenty of good courses which are incredible value. You can go instead to the likes of Hokitika, Takaka or Ahipara and pay less than one tenth of that price and still enjoy a great golfing experience.

Better still is to play those courses with members as members will give you an insight into the club as well as the course, as well as enabling you to enjoy golf as it should be played – with friendly competition. I am a great advocate of playing different golf courses with different people and with the escalating cost of green fees, paying members' guest rate is becoming the only affordable way to do so. Disappointingly, some clubs in the U.K. are pushing their members' guest rates to rather high levels. They used to be a perk of membership, allowing members to invite friends and show off their club. My late father was a member of Muirfield (he was not a great golfer but enjoyed going for lunch followed by usually just 9 holes of foursomes) but he could take me along for the princely sum of £5. That was not that long ago.

In saying that my trip has not given me any new insights, it has, however, confirmed a way forward for me, particularly for golf. I was enormously lucky on this trip to play the likes of Barnbougle Dunes, Cape Wickham, Jack's Point, Te Arai and Kauri Cliffs. These are all magnificent golf courses, each with its own characteristics and all a joy to play. Certainly, I have preferences, (in my opinion, Te Arai would win over Kauri Cliffs and Cape Wickham over Jack's

Point) but that is not the point. All are destination golf courses, to go and play and experience but they are not what golf is really all about. I played most of these famous courses alone (Te Aria was the exception and perhaps that was why I preferred it?) and I enjoyed them all. Playing solitary golf has its attractions. On each occasion, I actually had the course pretty much to myself which allowed me to explore the courses more and hit a few extra shots here and there. Awarding yourself a 'Mulligan' is one of the benefits of playing by yourself. Indeed, on one occasion I came to reflect on whether a birdie with a 'Mulligan' counts as a birdie? I put that out there for discussion though it is perhaps not something which the R&A Rules Committee should spend too much time on.

But the most enjoyable golf I played were the rounds at Tocumwal with Peter and his wife, my participation in the Saturday 'haggle' at Takaka partnering Warwick against Neil and Carl, and the threeball at Waiheke with Tom and Woody. And on reflection, the best distillery visits were those where I was able to talk directly with the owners, those who were creating the vision they had. In some respect the two places I got closest to this were at Fannys Bay with Mathew and Julie and at Waiheke with Mark.

I'm left to reflect that while whisky needs the scale investments which create the likes of Callington Mill and Cardrona and golf benefits from projects such as Barnbougle Dunes and Te Arai with celebrity course designers like Tom Doak and Bill Coore, the essence of both can be found elsewhere. The two key elements are people and place. Whisky can be enjoyed alone, allowing one quiet and solitary moments to reflect on life, but is better enjoyed with others, perhaps in the whisky bar of a distillery discussing the nuances of different products. Golf too can be enjoyed alone but serious fun is a competitive match on a bouncy seaside links for bragging rights in the bar afterwards, the result of which is forgotten twenty-four hours later. Going forward I will not eschew all destination golf courses and multinational owned whisky distilleries but I will certainly prioritise the smaller and the quirkier and always seek to share the experience with others.

BIBLIOGRAPHY

While there are numerous fine books on both whisky and golf the
following were particularly relevant to this book

Malt Whisky	*Charles MacLean*	**Lomond Books 2013**
Maclean's Miscellany of Whisky	*Charles MacLean*	**Little Books Ltd. 2015**
Malt Whisky Yearbook 2024		**MagDig Media 2023**
Whisky	*Aeneas Macdonald*	**Birlinn 2016**
A Sense of Place	*Dave Broom*	**Mitchell Beazley 2022**
The World Atlas of Whisky (3rd Edition) Dave Broom		**Mitchell Beazley 2024**
The Links	*Robert Hunter*	**Coventry House 2018**
Methods of early golf architecture Colt and A.W. Tillinghast	*The selected writings of Alister MacKenzie, H.S* **Coventry House Publishing 2013**	
The Spirit of St Andrews	*Alister MacKenzie*	**Broadway Books**
The Evolution of Golf Course Design	*Keith Cutten* **Full Swing Golf Publishing 2018**	
The Anatomy of a Golf Course	*Tom Doak*	**Burford Books 1992**

Printed in Dunstable, United Kingdom